JUST LOOK BACK

To: Brock!

Legacy is the road we build for others to walk on!.

You're Awesome!

- Joe

JUST LOOK BACK

Joe Beckman

ISBN 13: 978-1-63489-700-6

Library of Congress Catalog Number has been applied for.
Printed in the United States of America
First Printing: 2024

28 27 26 25 24   5 4 3 2 1

Cover design by Luke Bird
Interior design by Vivian Steckline and Patrick Maloney
Edited by Audrey Williams

Wise Ink
PO Box 580195
Minneapolis, MN 55458-0195

Wise Ink is a creative publishing agency for game-changers. Wise Ink authors uplift, inspire, and inform, and their titles support building a better and more equitable world. For more information, visit wiseink.com.

Since this book is about legacy, it only makes sense for me to dedicate the book and its ideas to two people who have been models of this word throughout my entire life. Mom . . . Dad . . . thank you.

For the big things like always having food on our table and clothes on our backs, your strong work ethic and love for your family allowed all of our basic needs to be met. In turn, this allowed our hearts to see how we could help meet the basic needs of others.

With that said, and you'll hear this refrain throughout this book, it's truly the small things that I appreciate the most.

The games of catch in the backyard.
The intense battles of Aggravation.
The plays you came to see me in.
The baseball teams you coached me on.
The road trips in the station wagon.
The Saturday night ritual of church, pizza, and WWF wrestling.

Each of these smaller moments plays a significant role in my larger story.

After two decades, now two books, and over two million people impacted, that story–centered around the power of human connection– continues to move forward. And the cool part is that you're with me every stop along the way. For every compliment I receive from others about how well I'm able to communicate a message or inspire some-one's heart, or how my talks have changed or saved someone's life, I think about you, and the road you built for Ann, Matt, and me.

Mom and Dad, I love you both more than you will ever know. My sincerest hope is that my children, Sophia, Finn, Jonah, and Gianna, will not only look back at their childhood with the same fondness as I do when I think of mine, but also see it as a road that they can start building their legacies upon.

I love you both so much.

Contents

Pre-Epilogue

*You are not a drop in the ocean; you
are the entire ocean in a drop.*

—Rumi

Okay, so. I know that "pre-epilogues" aren't real,
and starting an *entire book* of words with a fake word
might have you questioning my credentials.

The word felt appropriate, though. And not just because of my rule-breaking heart (which you will learn
a lot about in the coming pages).

In a way, this book starts at the end . . . or what I
thought was the end. It's both a prologue and an epi-
logue—the culmination of a big thing and the start of
something completely new.

x | JOE BECKMAN

See, I *do* know words. Would a guy who wasn't qualified to write a book use a word like "culmination"? Would a guy lacking book-writing credentials . . .

. . . have written a book before?

A Look Back at *Just Look Up*

Fine, I promise I'm done with that bit (but you were the one questioning 'pre-epilogue'!).

As weird as it feels to start one book by selling you on another (https://www.amazon.com/Just-Look-Up-Life-Saving-Phrases/), that story is an essential part of this one. I can't talk about building a legacy without talking about that journey.

In 2016, after years of speaking to students, administrators, and teachers with various organizations, I decided to start my own company. I did what everyone tells you not to do: I partnered up with family.

Clearly, I'm not opposed to bold, rule-breaking starts.

At the time, my wife's brother was living in the lower level of our house. Late one night, after my kids had gone to sleep, I went downstairs and told him *everything*.

Apparently, the late time of day made me feel even more empowered to dream.

I told him everything I wanted to create. The impact I felt that we could make.

And my knowledge that there was no way I could ever get there by myself.

He was willing to jump ship from his corporate job and take the risk with me. Things started very slow, but I focused on what I knew: people. By building connections, shaking hands, and making others feel important, everything began to change.

Schools were calling.

Conferences were booking.

Our schedule was filling.

Striking out on my own was scary, but it finally felt like I was making a name for myself.

It felt like a legacy.

Then . . . I met the big guy.

The Pontoon Principal

In 2019, I reached out to a "Curtis Slater" that I saw making waves on Twitter. We met up for coffee on his makeshift pontoon boat. He wore a shirt that read "I FIGHT for Kids"—a wholesome but intimidating message that was even more daunting when hanging on his 6'7" frame.

This was a man who meant business, and I was sure he was going to tell me how impressed he was with my work. I thought I would maybe even book a day of speaking at his elementary school.

Any good salesman knows how to take advantage of a captive audience. Right as we hit a cool three miles per hour cruising speed on the Mississippi River, I launched into my pitch.

Me: Have you seen any of the work that I've done, Curt?

Curt: Yup!

Me: (playing it cool, while simultaneously thinking that this is a slam-dunk) Nice, nice. What do you think?

Curt: You're good, but you're not that good. In fact, I would have never hired you to come to my school.

If a boat could skid to a stop, ours would have. And if I could've pushed him into the river, I *would* have . . . but did I mention he's 6'7"? I'm dumb, but I'm not stupid. I had no choice but to hear him out.

Curt: What happens after Joe Beckman? What are you providing my staff long-term? What are you providing my parents? Why on earth does it make sense that schools spend money on a speaker, only to get such little return on the investment? If you really want to make an impact, it's not about a day . . . it's about the next three to five years. That's what it takes to shift a culture.

Bam. His words hit me square between the eyes. Despite the growing success of the business, I knew something was missing. I knew that to have greater

xiv | JOE BECKMAN

impact, I needed to do more with the schools where I spoke, but I wasn't exactly sure how that should look. When Curt said this to me, it was clear: this was not only what my company needed and what schools needed, but also what it takes to build a legacy.

Suddenly, my team grew to three.

I know, I know. If going into a business with your family is a bad idea, then going into business with your family and a man that you briefly considered pushing out of a pontoon must be a *horrible* idea.

Fortunately, we got a fresh start. Scott, Curt, and I re-branded my solo speaking aspirations into TILL360.

TILL stands for Teach. Inspire. Listen. Learn.

360 represents that sometimes you have to completely turn things around if you truly want to help schools and districts move forward. We need to listen and learn before we *teach* and *inspire*.

The "360" also speaks to the fact that when we work with a district, our goal is whole-community learning. That means involving . . .

Students
Staff
Parents
Guardians
Outside community members

We know that for the best outcomes, we need all of these groups speaking the same language and working together.

TILL360 has grown, is growing, and (if Scott is crunching the numbers correctly) will continue to grow. We have employees, a robust video-based curriculum, a best-selling book, and . . .

Oh, yeah! I meant to tell you about the book!

The impact of *Just Look Up: Five Life-Saving Phrases Every Kid/Human Needs to Hear* was beyond anything we ever expected. We poured our hearts and souls into that book during the most disconnected, panicked, early months of the pandemic . . . and it's gone much further than we ever could have dreamed.

Our hope was to create a down-to-earth approach to finding self-worth (Love YOU), resilience (Push

Through), confidence (Fail On), joy (Yeah Toast!), and, perhaps most importantly, human connection (Just Look Up).

We hoped that it would sell five hundred copies, earning back our initial investment. Nearly three years later, the book has sold almost fifty thousand copies. It felt like the grand finale in everything I had been working toward.

I had taken years of experience and compiled everything I learned into a book that people were loving! The only one complaining was my teenage daughter . . . and even that turned out a bit positive.

[ENTER: Sophia Beckman, an eighth grader looking very annoyed—even for an eighth grader]

Sophia: It's *so* stupid.

Me: What's stupid?

Sophia: *Your* book.

Me: (having just donated a copy to her teacher) My book? Why is my book stupid?

Sophia: Because kids are fighting over it in my class!

In my earliest days of speaking to students, I never would've viewed inciting riots as a positive outcome. But this felt *great*.

I knew better than to think it felt like a legacy, though.

As the book spread around, we heard from readers of all ages. Educators, parents, accountants, lawyers, grandparents . . . they've all told us how important these concepts were to them too.

As it turns out, hitting a certain age—twenty or forty-two or eighty-seven—doesn't make life any less complicated.

The work never stops.

After all, *Just Look Up* was my compilation of everything I had learned.

But then I kept learning.

It might take me until book three to learn that "pre-epilogue" isn't a word. But I couldn't wait that long to invite you on this journey with me. I couldn't wait until the introduction to show you how our legacies are built in the everyday—in small interactions with our neighbors, in mundane moments that may feel like a waste, in the times we decide to move on. It's only in looking back that we can appreciate everything our legacy has been and will be.

Read that again! It's that important.

And then read it *again* to realize that . . . yes. This book has a pre-epilogue *and* an introduction.

Introduction

I was a freshman. Nervous, awkward, and walking down the hallway at my high school with a senior . . .

Scratch that.

THE senior.

Peter Malone, captain of the football team and Greek god, walked by me and said the three most glorious words a freshman could ever hear: "What's up, Beckman?"

The less important detail of this story is that I went to an all-male Catholic military high school, which required my name to be literally printed on a badge on my chest.

The *most* important detail is that a cool senior knew my last name!

Right next to other "amazing feelings in this world" such as . . .

- warm bed sheets out of the dryer,

- a fresh pair of underwear,

- snow days,

- finding $20 in your pocket,

- a clean garage,

- and the perfect barrel-to-ball connection from a fastball

lives . . .

- a cool high school senior knowing a freshman's last name.

But I understand that when it comes to knowing my name, you, on the other hand, might not (if you're the type of person who reads the introduction of a book before you read the cover).

Hi. My name is Joe.

I would never want to presume that readers of this book know anything about me. Unless, of course, you're Peter Malone. Then I'm a *little* bummed that

I no longer have the same status as freshman year me, but this is the perfect time to get reacquainted.

First things first: here's a virtual high-five. Truly, I would appreciate it if you would simply put your real hand in the real air and give me a fake high-five.

I'll wait.

Seriously, I've got all day. I wrote this months ago.

Well done!

As my middle-school-aged son, Finn, would say, "W."

Second: my name is Joe Beckman.

I say my last name for two reasons:

- My father, Mark Beckman, deserves an homage. He always approached every introduction with his first name, last name, and a firm handshake. The only thing tighter than his grip was the perm that he rocked when I was little.

- I got really, really lucky with my last name. Whether it's my closest friends, students I meet, or a stranger with whom I connect, "Joe Beckman" often turns into one word.

JoeBeckman.

Kind of like . . . BeYoncé or MaDonna. (I know you were wondering why I reminded you of these idols. This is just one of a few things we have in common . . . but I won't show off my singing until chapter 3.)

When you boil it down, I am a speaker by trade. Thanks to Curt Slater, my work has expanded a bit. But at my core, I'll always be a speaker.

My general work week looks like two to four days at either

- a school district,

- an educational conference, or

- a national speaking competition. I was once sand-wiched between Shark Tank's Robert Herjavec and Mark Wahlberg (Marky Mark for fans of the Funky Bunch). Tom Brady might drop dimes in the end zone, but he'll never be able to drop speaking creds like that. (Oh, yeah, the QB GOAT was there too.)

Speaker in Training!

Sometimes people say they "stumbled into this work." I honestly knew at a pretty young age that I had a love of storytelling and a heart for connection.

Of course, before I made it to the main stage, I had some smaller gigs. Again, much like Beyoncé, my solo career was fueled by my work in a group. Except, instead of Destiny's Child, I was a member of the Berenstain Bears.

Mama Bear, in particular. More on that later.

Still, looking back, I see that these smaller roles had their part in fueling my fire and building the legacy I had been working toward since I was a child. So step aside, Goldilocks—this part was *just right*.

(I may be getting my bear stories mixed up.)

In between small school gigs and raising my cubs, my mind started working. I picked up on small things that made the difference between a good performer and a great one.

- I learned how to use a microphone and music in a way that was able to control the energy in the room.

- I watched how some people could use comedy to win over even the least engaged students.

- I observed that no matter how energetic the groups got during games, a well told story could leave the room in captivated silence.

No matter how big a production was or the message we set out to tell, it was the little moments that would plant the seeds.

I know now that if we dismissed these little moments, if we forgot to look back at our seeds, we would never realize everything that we grew!

One of my first big speaking jobs involved putting on day-long retreats in schools. We would send messages about courage and speak against bullying.

It's a good thing we were actively training our audience in kindness . . . 'cause I *sucked*. Perhaps it speaks to the strength of the program that I wasn't hit with any tomatoes or booed out of the auditorium.

My presentation was rough. I was nervous, unpolished, and convinced that I wasted an entire day by failing to connect in any meaningful way with the students.

Then came a kiddo named Abdul.

I didn't know it at the time, but Abdul's little life had been *hard* so far. His story, though just getting started, was already pretty bleak.

I couldn't tell you what I told Abdul and his classmates that day. I was sure it was nothing of value. But I'll always remember what Abdul told me after the presentation:

"Mr. Joe . . . You make my heart so happy."

Evidently, I had given Abdul hope . . . and his words gave me an immeasurable boost of confidence. Despite how I felt about the rest of the day, I knew that I had at least touched one life. Planted one seed.

Twenty-five years later? Abdul is leading programming at the exact same company I worked for at the time.

Now *that's* growth.

The Road We're Building

When I'm speaking at elementary schools, I often ask students to share what they think of when they hear the word "legacy."

The responses are fascinating.

Besides an occasional mix-up with the word "destiny," kids are pretty dialed-in on this concept.

They say things like,

"Legacy is how you will be remembered!"
"Legacy is about the impact you make."
"My uncle's name is Joe!"

Not everyone is on-task all of the time. It's okay.

One time, a fifth-grade student raised his hand and said, "Legacy is like the road we build for others to walk on."

BOOM! Mind blown! That's it!

I don't know if the fifth graders had gotten to their metaphor unit yet in English, but this felt perfect. Picture a road—stretching forward and backward, with its bumps and detours and endless construction.

Think of all the people that help to build a road (even if it ends up being named after just one person).

Think of all the people that will one day drive on the roads you build, long after your own journey is over.

You are building that road

right now!
in this space!
at this time!

Roads require cooperation—trust in the people around you. Journeys are a lot less stressful when we believe in the good of people around us. Journeys *rely* on that nice guy in a Honda Civic occasionally letting us merge.

The idea of a road, with its concrete and rock, also speaks to the longevity we often think of alongside legacy. But new roads are being built all of the time!

It's never too late—or too early—to chart out a new path.

You're not lost or taking too long! This is the scenic route.

You haven't hit a dead end! This is just an invitation to strike out on foot.

Your work isn't done, that's just a stop sign! (And I'm the person behind you, about to lay on the horn.)

Even on the slow days, when you're stuck in traffic, you're on the road.

All of us . . .

Students
Teachers
Parents
Humans!

are on the road . . . the road that humans before us built . . . charting off to that far-off destination known as Legacy.

Five Keys for Unlocking Legacy

You didn't try to start a road trip without your *keys*, did you?

Don't worry, we've got you covered.

I'm not saying these are the only keys, but as I think about the road that I'm building, they are the ones that make the ring (let's be honest, unless you're a school custodian, you should have no more than five keys at any one time).

Your journey has been, currently is, and will continue to be different than mine . . . or anyone else's. We're all coming from different places, entering the journey at different points, and bringing different life experiences with us.

I'm not you, and I'm not trying to pretend to be you. (Unless, again, you're Peter Malone, high school football star. I have to admit—I'm still a little starstruck.)

I'm not naive enough to think I have everything perfectly figured out, and I can acknowledge how my own legacy has evolved in ways I never would have anticipated.

However, based on my experiences, I've gathered five important keys to hold onto as you navigate through this journey and continue to build your legacy . . . your road for others to walk/drive/bike/rollerblade (remember those?) on after you go. Together, we can look back to highlight the moments along the journey that make all the difference.

If I'm successful in my attempt to make sense here, one or two or maybe even all five of these phrases will resonate for you and the idea of your legacy. Sweet! That's step one.

Step two comes with a question.

"What are you going to do with it?"

This might sound like a challenge to what you've built so far. It might sound dismissive of what has already felt like a legacy. But wait—don't push me out of the pontoon yet.

The real test of this book isn't just to read it. It's to

do something with it. We'll end each chapter with a suggestion for how to do something with the key you've been given.

Our legacies—what we are known for when we are gone—will be built by our actions today.

So, yes,

read this book
soak in the stories
take in the wisdom
laugh at your incredibly witty narrator (aw, stop!)

But ultimately, do something with it. Because we need you. Our world needs you. Our communities need you. Our schools need you. Our kids need you.

We need *you* to bring your unique gifts to create a road that is strong enough for others to walk on after you're gone.

So thanks for joining me on this journey. In my experience these "longer trips" are always better with a companion or two...or 50,000. Keep an open mind and an open heart to th journey ahead, and never forget that it's never too late (or too early) to start building your road.

You're awesome!

—Joe Beckman

CHAPTER ONE

Seize the Season

I hate moving.

And I'm here to tell you that all of the traveling I do, with my work taking me state to state every week, does nothing to dull the hate I have for moving. Every part of moving—from planning to packing to unpacking and settling in—fills me with dread.

So it was a bittersweet feeling when, with the addition of our third child imminent, my family felt ready to build a bigger home.

Okay, yeah, it was mostly sweet. But the *moving*!

Deciding to build a home adds a lot of complicating factors to what is already an incredibly tedious task. You would think that taking the leap and choosing to build would be the hardest step.

Wrong.

Deciding that you're going to build is the easiest part of moving! As soon as you do that, though, you're faced with a million smaller, harder decisions and tasks that immediately negate any excitement that might come from a new house.

Like where do you want the outlets to be? Before you even have kitchen countertops, you need to think about where you're going to want to put your quesadilla maker and how you're going to plug it in.

(The second easiest part of moving is just deciding not to have a quesadilla maker. Let's be honest . . . a panini press does the same thing and has much more utility.)

Besides the parts of moving that are physically draining, making a move—literally or figuratively—is mentally and emotionally exhausting. Taking a step toward any big change is a declaration of faith in yourself and your future . . . and that's terrifying.

I have vivid memories of my first post-college apartment and the exciting moments that came with adult freedom. But aesthetically? It was sparse.

As exciting as it was to have my own place for the first time, I knew it was temporary. The furniture was worn and mismatched. I didn't bother hanging anything on the walls. It didn't matter that my panini press's cord would struggle to reach the rusty kitchen outlets—I didn't even have a panini press!

As I moved on, each place seemed to get a little more effort. In my first apartment with my wife, we took slightly more care in making a space that felt like ours. By the time we had our first home and kids, we were even so bold as to hang a picture or two on the wall!

I'm talking *hung* them. No Command strips here. This is our turf now.

It speaks to how much we all hate moving that even the act of settling in seems to be done with the next move in mind. In our first home, we were still buying used furniture and holding off on the dream items. When we did choose to invest in something, we were already considering how easy it would be to move to the next place.

This could be viewed as laziness . . . but I prefer to

think of it as optimism. Through every move, every box that was packed and unpacked into new houses, we kept our eyes fixed on home. We were never content to get fully settled, knowing there was a dream house we wanted to reach on the horizon.

This kind of optimism can be useful at first. The age-old advice to "Never settle!" is especially appealing when it can be used as an excuse to put off unpacking.

Still . . . while the idea of a temporary stay helped me to get through a year in a dingy post-grad apartment, our dismissal of what's "temporary" can start to blind us to the beauty of the everyday.

It can be easy to forget that a legacy isn't a moment—it's a lifetime.

And just as our legacies are never finished, we have to understand that there's never been an official beginning either. In fact, before we were even able to understand that the letter "L" was a consonant in our alphabet, we were on the way to creating our road.

If we spend too much time waiting for and planning on the dream home, or the dream career, or the accolade that will make us feel like we've finally "made it," we'll spend most of our lifetimes not feeling settled in. Not feeling at home in our own stories.

You might even spend nine years with a birdhouse in your bathroom.

Know What to Pack (and What's for the Birds)

Right around the time that I was being recognized as a freshman by a senior football star, my future wife was constructing hideous birdhouses in her home economics class.

Perhaps I'm being harsh.

Perhaps I should explain.

As we were in the process of decluttering our old home and getting it ready to sell, I came across an object that I had not seen since we had moved into the house almost a decade prior.

There was a birdhouse. Hanging in our main floor bathroom.

It was pretty standard—it had a wooden house-like structure that sat on top of a wooden trough for bird seed. On the top of the birdhouse was a length of cheap, frayed twine, carefully looped so that the feeder had something from which it could hang. You know, like on a branch on a tree. Outside. Where there are birds.

As a way to spruce it up a little bit, my wife had used gel paint to depict three different colored butterflies on the side of the house. In bright purple, green, and red, they seemed to declare, "This house is strictly for beautiful butterflies."

That was probably a confusing message for the birds. Even more confusing, though, was the fact that this all-inclusive butterfly/bird resort was *hanging in our indoor bathroom.*

In the same way that we seem to get nose-blind to the smells of our dog (but never the smells of our son's football cleats), I had become birdhouse blind. It didn't really "go" with the bathroom in any way, shape, or form. There was no bird theme, no butterflies, and the colors didn't come close to matching our decor.

In fact, the only thing that seemed to explain the birdhouse's place in our bathroom was the small hook in the ceiling from which it hung.

Evidently, nine years ago, something about that hook had called out to us. Maybe it said . . .

"Hey, looks like your hands are full from unpacking that box. Why don't you ditch the birdhouse here while you take those other homemade projects ~~to the garbage~~ to be hung on the fridge?" (Sorry, kids—the hook said it, not me.)

Or maybe . . .

"That birdhouse will be no match for Minnesota weather. Untreated wood and ancient home-ec paints won't last a single winter. I'll have to tell the bird building manager that things aren't up to code. You could be fined!"

However we had been hooked (literally), the birdhouse had somehow found its way to the bathroom. And stayed there.

For *nine* years!

Granted, when we first moved into that house, we hadn't known we'd stay for nine years. We weren't worried about designing a "forever" bathroom for a temporary house.

But plans change. Life happens. Almost a decade after that birdhouse made its way into our bathroom, our kids had grown up in that house. When they picture home, they'll imagine the place that my wife and I thought was just a pit stop.

Maybe the birdhouse doesn't seem like a big deal. After all, I stopped noticing it. But as I took it down from its hook, I couldn't help but think about wasted potential. Of all the objects, this is what we had hung onto. This is what had been displayed in a place we visited every day for nine years.

What could we have made this space if we had allowed ourselves to settle in?

It was then that I realized that packing isn't just about what we put in the boxes. It's about what we have the courage to leave behind.

As much as I can critique the structural integrity of

that birdhouse, it had already come pretty far. To reach that hook in our bathroom, it had survived all of Jess's previous moves—to say nothing of the fact that it even made it home from school! It had survived the fate of many report cards and permission slips, which seem to encounter wormholes on school buses that only my children can see.

At this point, could we really leave the birdhouse behind? Was this an inevitable piece of my legacy?

Nah.

Our constant focus on what is temporary and what is permanent can backfire in this way, too. We convince ourselves to stay stuck in our ways, just because we've already *been* stuck for so long.

Our obsession with making the next best move, and having it be perfect, can prevent us from ever moving at all.

And when we stop moving,
we stop growing
and stretching
and learning

and progressing.

We limit ourselves to what we know and lose the hunger and drive we once had. And what we know through lots of recent research is that continual growth is a key indicator of our personal happiness and mental wellness.

And I get it . . . at this point in the chapter some of you might be saying, "But, Joe, you're talking out of both sides of your mouth here. On one hand what I'm hearing is . . .

'Enjoy the present.
Live for today.
Stop constantly seeking what's next.'

"But at the same time I'm hearing you say . . .

'Move on from the old.
Push the limits.
Keep your heart focused on the future.'"

You're right. I'm saying both of those things.

The key is in the discernment process and how much

of our energy we put into both spaces. When we exclusively go to one side of the spectrum, we eliminate the possibility the other side brings.

So what's the magical balance? The answer is . . .

I have no idea . . . for you . . . at this moment.

The way I see it is that, just like in nature, there are different seasons in life. Each season requires a different amount of energy. And though they repeat, no season is ever the same, and because of that, we need to adjust.

The season you're in right now might be ripe with opportunities for growth! Maybe your kids are of an age where they don't need as much of your attention, or work shifts in a direction that requires new skill sets.

Or, on the other hand, you may be in a season where life is requiring all of your energy to be in the here and now. Maybe you have toddlers, or you are on a vacation with your family.

Maybe you're grieving someone or something, and

this season of your life is requiring you to be as rooted in the present as you possibly can be.

Wherever you are, each season requires us to go through the moving process. Similar to physically moving, we must choose what we want to keep, while at the same time making the conscious decision to leave certain things behind.

It takes work and thought and a whole bunch of self-awareness.
It takes heavy emotional lifting.
And no doubt it takes a group of people to support us in the process.

And with each season, we get another opportunity to recenter and recalibrate, to push the limits and dream big.

What season are you currently in? How long have you been there? Is it time to take a deep breath and take it all in, or is it time to step into something different?

And maybe most importantly . . .

What are you taking with you to the next season, and what do you need to leave behind?

The Summer I Turned Handy

The summer after my sophomore year in college, I headed to Alexandria, Minnesota, to participate in summer stock theater.

Stock theater is *intense*. You put on six shows in three months, so it's all hands on deck, all the time. When you're not cast in a show, you can bet that you'll be backstage, building the sets or running the lights.

That summer, I was cast in three out of six shows. When I wasn't learning my lines, I was learning how to use power tools to construct the backdrops for my fellow stars.

Summer flew by, but it was a crash course in basic construction. By the time all six shows had wrapped and we were taking our bows, I was about as comfortable using a drill as I was speaking on stage. It was a whole new skill set, and as it turned out, I was pretty good at it!

And? I didn't like it.

At one point, a young Joe Beckman might have clung to this new skill. I invested some time in it and seemed alright at it. Surely I needed to find a place for this temporary skill to create something permanently awesome in my life. Otherwise, isn't it just wasted time?

Actually, no. It's not.

Sometimes the purpose of a phase of life is to simply affirm where you want to get to in the long term.

During that summer, I settled into my role as a set builder so that I could enjoy the whole experience. But when I had an opportunity to move on, I did. Even as I had fun learning how to use new tools, I was reminded in every moment how much I loved being *on* stage.

When you're packing up for your next stage of life, it's okay to let some things go. It's not wasted time. You may not be bringing the birdhouse or the tools, but you'll always bring the lessons they taught you.

You'll go a lot farther, a lot faster, when you're not holding onto things you don't need anymore.

And when you need encouragement and proof of how far you've come, you can always go back.

You Can Go Home Again

No man ever steps in the same river twice, for it's not the same river and he's not the same man.

–Heraclitus

Everyone knows the phrase, "You can't go home again." It's that poignant but painful adage—home is a place you can't recover once you leave. Your childhood home will never live up to your childhood memories.

Not everyone knows the origin of the phrase. It was actually first the title of a 1940s book by Thomas Wolfe.

The book follows George Webber, an author who writes a story about his hometown. The book achieves massive success nationally . . . but the people from back home recognize themselves in the pages, and they don't like what they see. While the world celebrates him, George can't even go back home due to the death threats he's receiving.

Somehow, from this old story, instead of, "Try to be a little more subtle while gossiping about your neighbors," we derived the lesson of, "You can't go home again."

Look, I'm not trying to discredit the idea of not being able to return home (or at least to the place in your memories). This idea is so widely accepted that it's been retold through dozens of other clichés!

You can't go home again.
You never stand in the same river twice.
You can't turn back the clock.

But sometimes, I think the fact that we can't go home again—that the river never stops moving—is a good thing!

Building a legacy is a lot of work, but we don't have to put any effort into making time move forward. That'll happen no matter what! It's this passage of time that lets us look back at where we were and appreciate how far we've moved . . . even in the moments that felt slow.

Shift Happens

Like most college kids, I went home again for the holidays. After my first few months of studying and independence, winter break had arrived. I was so excited to head home and reconnect with one of my best friends, Clint.

You'll hear about Clint a whole bunch in this book because he was my childhood best friend. Though the story I'm about to share might make Clint sound like a bad person, believe me when I tell you that he is a gem of a human and, amazingly, still one of my best friends to this day.

I say "amazingly" because, let's be honest, picking childhood friends is probably less about true compatibility and more about who lives down the block. Clint and I became best friends because we ran into each other at a friend-making age. We stayed best friends because . . . we were best friends!

When it came time for college, we went our separate

ways. Clint headed off to a different school, and now, at winter break, I was eagerly anticipating our reunion.

Unfortunately, Thomas Wolfe didn't prepare me. It's not just home that feels different than you remember; it's the homies too.

During our first time hanging out back at home, Clint made a joke. For all I know, it could've been a classic Clint joke . . . but it rang differently in my ears. It was crass. It was crude. It wasn't funny at all.

"Dude . . . not cool," I said.

Clint looked just as baffled as I felt. Evidently, he had been expecting laughter. After a bit of awkward silence, he shook his head disappointedly. "You've changed," he said.

Maybe I had. I felt far removed from the type of person who would laugh at that joke, the type of person that Clint seemed to think I was. But I couldn't convince myself of that being a bad thing.

"The problem isn't that I've changed, Clint," I finally said. "It's that you haven't."

It's never easy to outgrow a friend, or to realize that your high school self had a questionable sense of humor. At the time, my conversation with Clint didn't feel like a victory. It felt awkward. It felt like I couldn't trust my fond memories of my friendship and home.

With a bit more time and perspective, though, this changed. It started to feel like proof.

The first few months of college aren't easy. Sure, the newfound independence is fun. The cafeteria food hasn't yet lost its appeal. But . . .

things are slow-moving.
Friendships are tentative and shy.
Your whole schedule is your "generals."

Before I came home for winter break, I didn't feel like I was making any progress. A degree and a job and meaningful work felt a long way off.

With one conversation, Clint proved that, day-to-day, I was making movement toward who I wanted to be. Going back home affirmed that I no longer fully fit there. I was ready to break into a new space.

Later in college, I would have the opportunity to surprise myself again. I took that first step into the river (that I would never be able to stand in again!) by studying abroad.

Greco-Roman Studying

Alongside a group of peers, I spent six weeks in Greece and six weeks in Rome. One of my "peers" was slightly more than that—I didn't know that Jess was my future wife yet, but she was absolutely my girlfriend . . . despite what we told the group leaders.

Our school had a rule against couples going on the same study abroad trip. Evidently, there were concerns that a mid-trip breakup would ruin the vibes. What they *didn't* realize was that forcing Jess and I to *secretly* date in Europe would only add to the romance.

On the weekends, free from classes, we could take advantage of Europe's inexpensive travel between its tightly packed countries and use public transportation to explore famous cities on our own. Of course, this freedom was slightly limited by our status as broke college students, but we still had fun.

I'll never forget the fine dining we did in a London train station . . . eating free saltines and jelly packets while I left my hat out for spare change, hoping to earn our fare home.

Perhaps it was the magical meals or perhaps it was to spite our teachers, but Jess and I did not break up on that trip. In fact, our relationship even lasted long enough for us to return years later.

Look, not to keep disproving beloved clichés, but our return to Greece proved to me that old Heraclitus got the first part of his river quote wrong. And he was Greek!

The fun thing about visiting ancient cities is that they largely *do* stay the same. It's the same river! The same Parthenon and Acropolis. Recreating our study abroad trip had us capturing the same iconic landmarks (on slightly better cameras) and learning the same old history from tour guides.

He was right about one thing, though: I was not the same man.

Italy and Greece were worth returning to, not just because they're incredible countries. Taking the time to revisit that college trip allowed Jess and me to see just how far we had come. We walked the city with slightly more money in our pockets. Slightly more confidence in ourselves.

We could afford our train station saltines! (They were free like last time, but still!)

When I proposed in Italy, I was *grateful* for how much had changed.

And how much had stayed exactly the same.

When you're moving houses, you know what you're packing for. At least, mostly.

You know what address to give the U-Haul driver. You have the new keys made.

In the same way, I thought I knew what I was packing for when I filled my study abroad suitcase all those years ago. I put the luggage tag on. I thought that the end goal was baggage claim.

Until I gave things time, kept it moving, and finally looked back . . . I never realized just how far that trip really took me.

Get a Move On! (But Settle In)

I still hate moving. Some days, throughout the home-building journey, the only thing that kept me packing boxes was imagining my family settling into our new place.

It's a lot harder to get through a move when you don't know where you'll end up. But legacy-building doesn't have to wait until you know the end.

Throughout every one of life's moves, you're gathering the skills, lessons, and people you'll need to settle into your "dream house." To construct your legacy.

You might not be able to see the kitchen yet. You might not be able to even *imagine* the panini press. But I promise . . .

With every packed box and leap of faith, you're building the foundation.

The more comfortable we get with moving, the less we have to fear an uncertain future.

Granted, the future will always be a little scary . . . but the better we get at packing up our memories, lessons, and hopes for the future, the easier it'll be to navigate life's twists and turns.

Reflect on this season of life.
Own the space you're in right now.
Unpack where you're at.

Home is where your heart is . . . so give your all to this moment.

And at the same time . . .
Keep an eye on what's next.
Challenge yourself to grow.
Say "yes" to as many opportunities you have that support the season of life you are currently in.

Remember . . . all of this is a "yes, and" not an "either, or."

"Yes"

to taking time to reflect on the season you are in, and the road that you have built

"And"
challenging yourself to keep building your road—a road that others are walking on behind you—as long and wide as you can.

Seize the Season!

Caveman Wisdoms: Legacy Edition

In the first book, Just Look Up, *I end each chapter with something I call "Caveman Wisdoms." These are the suggestions for activities or ways of thinking that are small steps in the right direction to help you put into action the ideas presented in each chapter. Many of them help you build habits that strengthen your connection to others.*

Why mess with a good thing? This book will also include "Caveman Wisdoms," but this time, they will be focused on the little things you can do to actively create a legacy of which you will be proud.

Nearly all of us have "that" drawer. You know the one. It has:

a ticket stub from that movie you saw last summer,
a container of safety pins,
a thank-you note from that graduation gift you sent,
your nieces' last-year school pictures,
an Allen wrench, and
sixteen charging cords for devices you may or may
not still own

shoved in haphazardly. There's a chance it barely closes. For some of us, the clutter may stop at one junk drawer. For others, it may extend beyond that to untidy piles on our desks, cluttered kitchen counters, and a messy room full of clothes on the floor.

(Or, ahem, a birdhouse hanging on a hook in your bathroom.)

Whether you consciously realize it or not, this disorganization affects you. When your physical space is cluttered, so is your mental and emotional space . . . and it can really be dragging you down.

Don't believe me? There's actually a lot of research that proves this! A summary of several studies[1] indicates that cluttered spaces can

---

1   Martinez, Shandra. "The Science Behind Decluttering." MI Blues

increase levels of cortisol (that pesky stress hormone),
increase negative feelings, and
decrease our productivity.

My solution here isn't simply telling you to tidy everything up all at once, and magically, everything will be easier for you. Clutter happens for a lot of reasons, and it usually happens over a long period of time due to habits and schedules and life. I get it . . . there's no judgment here.

No, instead, my suggestion here is that you focus on one area of clutter. Maybe it's your junk drawer. Maybe it's that random pile of socks that have lost their mate in the laundry, taking up valuable space by your washing machine. You know what first came to mind when you started reading this chapter . . . go with that.

Commit to cleaning it up,
Declare to declutter.
Testify to tidiness.

Throw out what you don't need, donate what could

Perspectives, September 9, 2021, https://www.mibluesperspectives.com/stories/mental-health/the-science-behind-decluttering.

still be useful to someone else, and organize what remains that you need to keep.

Not only will the end result benefit you, there's also research to suggest that the work of decluttering can provide you with a mood boost in the moment as well! Doing something active with your body while your mind gets a chance to relax can have a positive effect on your overall mental health.

And that's what we're after here . . . activities and habit-building that free you, so you can more actively engage with those around you in those small, legacy-building moments that matter.

CHAPTER TWO

Undercover Angels

I've always loved an underdog story.

Or, perhaps more accurately, I've always *rooted* for the underdog. I can't say that I routinely love their stories . . . especially when things don't work out in their favor.

Every December during my childhood, the Beckman family would gather in my grandmother's basement (her name was Cutie Pie for what it's worth) to watch any one of a number of holiday classics.

With a raffle ticket at her VFW, Cutie Pie evidently won a movie-playing device one year called a VHD.

Picture an old-school VCR *(be kind, rewind)* and a new(er) school Blu-Ray, and now replace the small Blu-Ray disc with a large record. And instead of simply placing the disc in the machine, you had to insert the entire case!

Along with the machine itself, Cutie Pie won ten free movies. You know, so she could give it a test run . . . with her grandchildren.

Cutie Pie was many things . . .

Avid bowler
Blatz beer drinker
Bingo dauber

But film aficionado was not one of them.

Maybe it was the Blatz talking, but Cutie Pie curated a VHD library that consisted mostly of Chevy Chase and Sylvester Stallone.

Rocky IV
Rambo II: First Blood
National Lampoon's European Vacation

were some of the crowd favorites.

One year, as a gift, she was given the holiday classic, *A Christmas Story.* Although the entire movie foreshadows Ralphie "shooting his eye out," the moment I remembered most was the *triple dog dare*.

For those who aren't familiar with the 1980s hallmark of Christmas cinema: a small plot feature of *A Christmas Story* involves a young boy, Flick, being triple-dog dared to lick a flagpole outside of the school.

If you're familiar with the bitter cold of Midwest winters, you know this is a horrible idea.

And if you're familiar with triple dog dares, you know that it wasn't optional.

When Flick's tongue quickly freezes to the pole, my young heart would break. While my family laughed at his iconic cries of, "It'th thtuck!" I would have to shield my eyes.

While I'd like to think that I would never fall for this wintry prank, I could relate to Flick in other ways. Being the youngest of three, I often felt like the runt of the litter or the third wheel.

When I saw that little boy give into a dare to try to win brownie points with his peers, I saw myself. There are still some days where I wake up feeling like Flick, and flinch away from every flagpole.

I thought I was fairly well-adjusted and resigned to my place in the family. There's no shame in being the third wheel!

Though every Christmas would remind me of my status as an underdog, this sentiment was offset by every Saturday. Blessedly, Saturdays occur much more frequently and allowed me to visit a person who helped me to break out of my lowly third-child funk and realize my potential.

Pick-Me-Up on Aisle Three

Growing up, Saturdays were one of my favorite days of the week.

This might seem like a fairly basic choice, but I feel pretty unique in my reasoning.

Sure, Saturday has the advantage of no school or work. It also lacks the feeling of dread that accompanies Sunday's proximity to Monday. On Saturday, you could kick back, relax, and anticipate the NFL games on the horizon.

Saturdays were *extra* special in the Beckman

household though. You see, this sacred weekend day was also when my mom would do the weekly grocery shopping. One of the three kids would get chosen at random to accompany her to Rainbow Foods, helping to push the carts that would transport our haul.

We also got to be assistant baggers at the end of the trip. My '80s childhood was training for the modern-day self-checkout era.

Now, you might think that a day of cart-pushing and bag-filling sounds horrible to a kid. It's true that my buddies were often out on their bikes, riding around and playing pick-up games of baseball.

You would be wrong, though.

For young Joe, there was a weekend prize that was even more valuable than freedom: free food.

Saturday was sample day at Rainbow Foods.

The workers at the sample station weren't some new trainees, serving up scraps. Rainbow Foods was stocked with a whole army of food-sampling ninjas.

Okay, yes—they were mostly senior citizens. But grandmas are notorious for making sure their grand-children are well fed! Truly, there was no better de-mographic for the job.

They were stationed strategically around the store with the latest cooking technology, sampling differ-ent products and preparation techniques in nearly every other aisle.

Some Saturdays, I would load up on tortilla chips and salsa. Other days featured mini-weenies with BBQ sauce, or hot pizza that they cooked right in front of you! It was well worth the wait.

For an eight-year-old, poking my head into each aisle provided the same adrenaline rush as pulling the le-ver of a slot machine. You never knew what would pop up next!

One thing was consistent about Rainbow Foods, though, and that was Patsy.

Patsy worked in the checkout, and I always got ex-cited when my mom chose her line.

Not because I was eagerly anticipating my post-shop bagging duties. (I wasn't.)

Not because I loved pressing the button that controlled the belt and moved the groceries up. (I most certainly did.)

Not because I had the day free to get on my bike and do whatever my heart desired after we got home. (I definitely would, the minute I got home from the grocery store.)

The true anticipation came from seeing Patsy.

Patsy was, hands-down, the most "senior" member of the team. Although her lines were always the longest, it didn't matter. We would've waited all day for Patsy.

Plus, her line came with a show!

I would watch in awe as Patsy would, no-look style, run each item through her fancy UPC reading machine. She made eye contact with the customer and smiled the entire time.

As soon as we joined her line, my eyes would stay glued to Patsy. Even if we were a couple customers back and I had to crane my neck, I wouldn't glance away. I didn't want to miss the moment that Patsy noticed me and did what she always did.

Stop mid-sentence,
tilt her head,
and look at me, wide-eyed and open-mouthed, as if she were seeing her favorite rockstar.

I loved that look!

Finally, when it was our turn to check out, she would exit her station, walk around, get down on a knee, and hug me as tight as she could.

Often she would say, "My goodness, Joey. You are getting so big! You are a special, special young boy. Do you know that?"

And I would say, "Yes." Every time.

I can still see her face.
I can still feel that squeeze.
I can still hear that voice.

You are a special, special young boy.

I may have spent Christmas relating to the underdog, but every Saturday was a reminder of what I could be.

I wasn't the underdog. I wasn't a mini-weenie with BBQ sauce. I could be the overdog! I could be seen as great *and* do great things.

I think I just needed someone to confirm it for me.

Kindness Undercover

At eight, I hadn't yet mastered the art of attaching legacy-defining titles to moments like those in the grocery store. All I knew was that my interactions with Patsy made me feel on top of the world . . . and that's a feeling that I wanted to recreate for others.

One of the highlights of my work speaking in schools has been the opportunity to share this message with the "littles"—pre-K, kindergarten, first and second graders.

What's amazing about this age is the spectacular lens of wonder and awe through which they see the world. The same childhood spirit that guided Joe through the maze of grocery store aisles, in pursuit of free samples, exists in the kids today.

Scaffolded around everything their little brains are learning in school is the strong belief that every dream and desire of their hearts is possible. They're reading their first stories and are still confident that they are the main character in their own.

A great privilege of my job is getting to confirm this inkling for them.

As I learned first-hand from my encounters with Patsy, grown-ups have the power to validate kids' biggest hopes and strongest suspicions. When a first grader hears that they're great from someone who's walked a few more miles down the road of life, it can be a light-bulb moment.

"You mean YOU see something special in ME? That same sort of special that I already sort of believe to be true?"

Game changer.

As I reflected upon all of the people who have done this for me in their own way, I stumbled upon a phrase that seems to succinctly define who those people in our lives are: Undercover Angels.

There are three things about them that I know to be true.

1. They are often people who, on the surface, play an insignificant role in our lives—hence the "undercover."

2. They surround us and are present in most places we go. We might not always be paying attention, but they're always there.

3. Their support can take you anywhere and their impact never expires (just like airline miles!).

Once you start thinking about Undercover Angels, you might start to see them (and their impact) everywhere! The legacy you're building now is likely supported by a foundation of angels.

Think of . . .

An educator who saw something in you that no one else did and, for the first time, you believed in yourself in a way that you hadn't before.

The coach who gave you a shot to do something you didn't think you were capable of. By pushing you outside your comfort zone, they helped you prove your own strength.

Or maybe it was

a friend's parent,
or a volunteer at your church,
or a grocery store clerk.

If you're a bit older, you might have recently encountered an angel in the form of

the stranger you sat next to on a plane,
the parent you chatted with at your kid's baseball game,
or your urinal buddy in the men's bathroom.

Kidding! Urinal buddies are not Undercover Angels—they're under-clothed devils, and they don't get a chapter in this book. Human Law #43: Thou shalt not talk to another human in the bathroom.

Humans may have a lot of laws, but being an angel is quite simple. Just as someone can serve as an angel for you without even knowing it, you can be an angel for others in your everyday actions.

You can even be an angel for someone else at the same time that they're being an angel for you! It's that easy.

You certainly don't have to be a speaker to make that difference for someone. Patsy did it from the grocery store line. And if you think being and seeing angels can't be as routine as your daily commute, let me tell you about a public transportation encounter that changed my life.

Heaven or "L"

My senior year of high school, I was faced with a big decision. Bigger than deciding where I would go to college, or who I would room with my freshman year.

Those were low stakes.

My big concern, with graduation on the horizon, was: Where am I gonna go for spring break?!

I was presented with two options at around the same

time. Clint was going to Mexico. It was set to be the quintessential high school spring break—a week of beaches, no supervision, and a legal drinking age of eighteen.

I readily agreed to go.

Later that same day, though, I ran into one of my favorite teachers. Mr. Mullen was organizing a service trip to the south side of Chicago.

"I think you'd be great for this," he told me. "Plus, it's the perfect addition for college applications."

Mr. Mullen was definitely an undercover angel in my life. While my parents were hoping I wouldn't get into too much trouble over spring break, Mr. Mullen believed that I could make a real difference with that week.

So, with the selfless heart for service that all eighteen-year-old boys possess . . .

I picked Mexico.

I know, I know.

Fortunately, Clint turned out to be an undercover angel in his own right. Eighteen-year-olds may not be known for their love of volunteering, but they're also notoriously poor planners. Mexico fell through, and I soon found myself en route to Chicago, with seven virtual strangers.

It may have been my second choice, but I'm also a pretty optimistic guy. As soon as we left for our mission, I had dramatic visions of how our group would transform Chicago—prompting instantaneous change and probably earning a key to the city.

I was ready to flex those angel wings!

Throughout the week, we worked as volunteers with many cool organizations. It was certainly a worthwhile trip, and I learned a lot. I still didn't feel as though I had that aha moment though.

I didn't need to save the day or make a moment about my individual action. We had grown together as a group, and I knew we were stronger together. But as we ate our last dinner and boarded the "L"— the system of trains that travel the city on an elevated track—to return to our hotel for one last night, it felt like something was missing. All week, I had built up energy and a belief in the power to inspire change. Now I just had to go home?

Okay—maybe I'm prescribing too much introspection to my young self. These thoughts were probably lingering in the back of my mind, but I mostly spent that train ride being an absolute teenage menace with my new friends.

In our week in Chicago, we had grown accustomed to taking the "L." With the boldness of locals, we now had a car to ourselves and were hanging from bars, hopping from seat to seat.

We were a few stops from our destination when the train rolled to a stop and the doors opened. My classmates and I rapidly fell into our seats, trying to appear casual and well-behaved for whoever was about to join our party car.

A single woman slowly ambled on, pushing a shopping cart. We fell silent and averted our gaze as she moved to her own row of seats. As the train restarted, our conversation remained paused.

It was in this silence that we heard the woman begin to cry.

Look down, Joe.

It was an immediate instinct. A million thoughts were rushing through my head:

There's not anything I could do to help.
All of my classmates are just ignoring her.
No one likes to be seen crying—I'm doing her a favor by pretending she's not there!

Look down, Joe.

What could I, an eighteen-year-old kid, offer a woman who was experiencing such immense pain? Who appeared, if not homeless, then entirely hopeless?

If I couldn't even imagine how she was feeling, how could I possibly come up with a way to help?

Look down, Joe.

Except, as I stared at my shoes, which had traveled

all over Chicago for the past week . . . I found that I could imagine how she might be feeling.

I looked at her cart and thought of my trips with my mom—when we would use two whole carts just for our weekly groceries. Her one cart appeared to hold all of her worldly possessions.

I thought of squeaky wheels and narrow aisles, and I couldn't imagine navigating my life onto the "L" in front of a bunch of teenagers.

I remembered the routine of getting to see Patsy catch my eye in line. This woman had probably grown used to eyes falling away.

I found myself standing up and moving toward her. Mr. Mullen noticed the movement and quickly stuck out his arm.

"What are you doing, Joe?" he whispered in a bit of a panic. Evidently, our trip permission slip didn't have a contingency for talking to strangers on the "L," and he didn't know what would come of this encounter.

I moved past him, though, and took a seat next to

the woman. Before I could question myself or let the potential judgment of my peers change my mind, I wrapped my arm around her.

She slowly leaned into me as she cried a little harder. We stayed like that until her stop arrived and she left the train.

I'd like to think that I helped her that day, in some little way. I hope that her tears picked up pace when I sat with her because she felt some relief at being seen, or perhaps felt the comfort she needed to truly let go.

But the thing to remember as Undercover Angels is . . .
We don't get to choose what kind of impact we have.

I don't know how that woman looks back at that day. I don't know if my classmates took something from that experience. I only know that I did my best with what I had, and I hoped that the ripples would end up someplace positive.

That woman was certainly an undercover angel for me. She strengthened my heart for connection and validated my hopes of being a source of comfort for others. She trusted me enough, as a stranger, with her tears.

Most of all, she taught me that you don't have to be in the perfect place to make a difference. So many of us put off using our angel magic until we feel like we've "arrived." But we weaken our legacy by not viewing *every single day* as an opportunity to build it.

You don't have to be on a service trip to serve others.

You don't even have to know how you're helping to help others!

Simply acting with a pure heart and kindness might lead you to surprising places.

Next Stop: Bear Country

Long after I left Chicago and the "L," all roads would continue to lead to the Bears. I just didn't know it yet.

After navigating the essential decision of where to spend my spring break, it was finally time to start thinking about college. My mom called a family meeting. (Though we were the only two people in the house. I think that's more appropriately called a conversation . . . or a confrontation.)

She was feeling slightly put off by my plans of being a theater major. A notoriously frugal woman, she didn't like the odds of my degree allowing me to eventually move out of her home and support myself.

As we debated at the kitchen table, I'm guessing she thought she was being an undercover angel.

Sometimes, people just need to hear the hard truth.
This will be better for him in the long run!
Mothers know best.

She wasn't entirely wrong! While I disagree with the entire internal monologue I've recreated for her, she *was* being an undercover angel. Just not in the way she meant to.

You see, my mom's resistance to my theater major aspirations transformed me . . . from an undecided freshman who was leaning toward theater to a formally declared thespian.

Sometimes, you just need someone to tell you that you *can't* to fully believe that you can.

Especially when you're a teenager and that "someone" is your mom.

I began auditioning for everything, eager to land a gig and prove my acting chops. I was constantly on the lookout for opportunities, and one day, I spotted a call for auditions in an unsuspecting place: my local coffee shop.

I was initially a little suspicious. The poster was looking for actors to work at Valley Fair, a nearby amusement park.

Their roller coasters seemed like a good place to practice my screaming should I ever land a horror movie, but I wasn't sure that was a job. Still, I called the number.

As it turned out, Valley Fair had recently begun hiring entertainers to perform skits, songs, and dances around the park—providing a different form of fun for those who needed a break from the long lines and coasters.

I needed a summer job, and an amusement park didn't seem like the worst way to spend the summer, so I auditioned.

Weeks went by with no call. Finally, just as I was beginning to lose hope, my phone rang.

This was it! This was my undercover angel—the one person I needed to see my potential and provide my big break.

My Hero: Hi, is this Joe Beckman?

Me: (practicing my acting skills by pretending to be totally chill) Yeah, hi!

My Hero: I'm with Valley Fair. We really appreciated your audition and we're interested in offering you a job here.

Me: That's amazing! Am I going to be one of the singers?

My Hero: Um, no. Not this time around.

Me: (with equal enthusiasm) A dancer?

My Hero: Not quite.

Me: Oh . . . ?

My Hero: (no longer living up to his name) This summer we're launching a new section in the park for families called Berenstain Bear Country. We're hoping you can be part of its inaugural staff.

Me: (wondering if minimum wage is worth the risk of being mauled by bears) Okay . . .

My Hero: I assume you're familiar with the Berenstain Bears?

Me: Oh! Of course! Will I be playing Papa Bear?

My Hero: Well . . . you see . . .

Me: Brother Bear?

My Hero: He's been cast.

Me: Surely not Sister Bear?

My Hero: Ha, no. Not Sister Bear.

Me: That means . . .

I may have ignored my mom's career advice, but I was still somehow going to be following in her footsteps. I was about to spend a summer . . . as Mama Bear.

It wasn't the breakout role I had been envisioning, but I quickly came to terms with it. After all, this could just be a stepping stone. If I proved myself this summer, maybe I'd get a better part next year.

Besides, my ego was spared by the fact that I didn't actually have to show my face as Mama Bear. The costume for this starring role was a full-body bear suit—polka dots, collar, and all.

Aside from the stifling summer humidity, it was a fairly cushy gig (literally). And before you ask about my Mama Bear voice, I'll tell you: I didn't even have to talk!

Though Valley Fair saw my potential to be a female bear, they did not trust me to voice her. Each bear was equipped with a "handler" who also served as our interpreter. They would lean up to our fuzzy faces, pretend to listen, and answer children's questions for us.

I know what you're thinking. *Joe, is that really an acting job if you didn't even have to talk?*

I'll have you know that a bear's personality shines through its *actions*. There's a reason it's called a "bear hug" and not a "bear hype speech."

There were still plenty of times I had to think on my feet. The days were long, the parks were crowded, and there were plenty of tiny, Undercover Angels running underfoot.

One day, I got separated from my interpreter. A young park visitor came running up to me, poking my fluffy side.

"Mama Bear!" she said in a quiet but squeaky voice. "Mama Bear!"

For some kids, surprised jazz hands and a wave just aren't gonna cut it.

"Mama Bear!" she tried again. "I'm hungry!"

And I'm a man in a woman's bear suit. Sometimes being undercover isn't the most effective way to help people.

Still, I was nothing if not a method actor. I remained silent and simply offered the only thing I could: a classic Mama Bear hug. She accepted, but I could almost feel her disdain.

Like, okayyy. But what's this gonna do about my hunger?

She scampered off to find someone who could offer a more relevant solution. But she left me with a very important lesson.

I could've taken that summer as a sign of defeat. I could've reconsidered my mom's warning, and interpreted it in the way that she wanted.

But as I looked at the kids smiling all around me, I felt as though I was exactly where I should be. I found fulfillment in making other people smile. I felt lucky to be in a position to wave and give high-fives and be a part of making dreams come true. It was a privilege to be the matriarch of Bear Country.

Caveman Wisdoms: Legacy Edition
You Had Me at Halo

Those people and that lesson—just like the smell of the inside of that bear suit by the end of summer—will stay with me forever. That's the power of an Undercover Angel. They stay with you forever.

By this point, it's hopefully clear that Undercover Angels can be found everywhere—from the grocery store to the "L" and Bear Country. You might even be eagerly anticipating your next shopping trip so that you can spot an angel and bask in their glow.

I'm guessing that you started identifying your own Undercover Angels as you read through these stories. How quickly could you reach out to them? How could you connect with their friends and family if they've passed n, reminding them of their loved one's legacy?

I bet you could do it in less than a minute.

I recently read a study about gratitude. There's persuasive data that suggests practicing gratitude has myriad short- and long-term benefits. These include, but are not limited to:

- Reduced stress

- Improved self-worth

- Free trips to Mexico

Just checking to make sure you're still paying attention.

And just like you can be an angel for someone while they're being an angel for you, expressing gratitude for someone who's helped you can help them!

It's as easy as telling someone they've made an impact.

According to the study, the moment we realize that we've been an Undercover Angel for someone else, that our words or actions or energy are even the smallest part of someone else's story, two amazing things happen.

1. Our bodies experience a rush of positive chemicals (hola, serotonin and oxytocin!).

2. Negative chemicals that are wasting space are

significantly reduced (peace out, cortisol, you've been kicked to the curb twice now).

If you thought that the best holiday gift for your kid's teacher was a $25 gift card to the closest liquor store, guess again.

Simply by . . .

typing a quick email
crafting a short text
writing a handwritten note
making a call

. . . we are giving that person a gift they will feel the benefits from, potentially for the rest of their lives.

(Maybe still throw in the gift card, though. Teaching is hard work.)

What if you started each day this way? Racking your brain and reconnecting with the people who have laid the foundation for your legacy?

Think of the stress you could reduce. Think of the good vibes and happy chemicals you could channel all over the world. Think of all the effort, energy, and intention that you could put into looking for Undercover Angels and the goodness they have brought to your life.

With all that thinking focused in such a positive direction, not only will you see the Undercover Angels in your own life, but maybe more importantly, you'll see that there are so many different ways that you can be an Undercover Angel for others.

Go be an Undercover Angel.

I triple dog dare ya.

CHAPTER THREE

Embrace Boredom

I was a pretty happy kid most days of the week. You can ask any classmate, parent, grandparent, neighbor, or stranger in the grocery store, and they'll tell you the same thing! (Or perhaps, if you're not shopping at my childhood grocery store, they'll look at you with some confusion.)

Somewhere from conception to birth—and probably in part because of my mom's copious cravings for fast-food strawberry milkshakes during pregnancy—I was injected with the "happy gene."

I seemed to approach every single day with endless enthusiasm. Even on weekends, I would wake early to soak up the day's potential. This was especially true on Saturdays. As any adult reading this knows, there was a time before Netflix, Disney+, and all of those other streaming services that put dozens of cartoons at the tip of our fingers. Before those . . . all we had was Saturday morning.

Some days, I'd be so excited that I'd wake up even *earlier* than the cartoons' start time. Ever in the pursuit of vanquishing boredom, I'd tune into the finest programming that early mornings had to offer.

Infomercials!

Let's just say that one of my life's more minor Undercover Angels is Ron Popeil.

I would watch Master Ron himself take thin slices of meat and stick them into a circular, new-age giant capsule and turn them into beef jerky . . .

Stare deeply into Tony Little's eyes while he screamed about his new fitness machine, "The Gazelle" . . .

Listen to the sweet sounds from a series of cassette tapes entitled "The Secret Love Album"—forty-eight soft rock classics by the original artists . . .

But wait, there's more!

If the infomercials weren't managing to occupy all of my attention, these slow Saturday mornings were the perfect time to plan out my days. I was always on the lookout for any and all opportunities to get on my bike, meet up with friends, or even make a little money.

The summer between my sixth- and seventh-grade years, I caught wind of a summer job that would allow me to make roughly $5 an hour. This was a huge raise from what my previous endeavors yielded.

(Evidently, there wasn't a huge market looking to purchase the cool rocks I found in the woods, and my Kool-Aid stand's income hardly covered the cost of each cup's heaping spoonfuls of sugar.)

This new job—my big break!—was decidedly more profitable and glamorous. This was to be the summer of . . . caddying.

If I could wake up at 6:00 a.m., carry around a bag of golf clubs, and develop the patience to deal with privileged club members, I could conquer my boredom to the tune of $18 per eighteen holes.

Sign. Me. Up.

The Caddyshack

I have to tell you a story about a shack . . . a funky little shack. It was set really far in the back or middle of some field, and man, everyone always wanted to get back to it!

Sorry, did you think I was talking about the famous love shack from that old B-52's song? Nope, I was referencing another famous shack from 1980s pop culture: Caddyshack. And guess what? Caddyshack wasn't just an incredible movie. It was a real thing!

In the case of the Somerset golf course, you couldn't be blamed for missing this magical place. Our caddyshack was nestled right on the edge of the 7th hole green and the 8th hole tee box, as far away from the main entrance as possible, in a nearly empty old lot. It was the home to two distinguishing landmarks: a rusty basketball hoop with a bent rim and ripped net, and a decrepit stone shack with zero windows, zero bathrooms, and, best of all, zero adult supervision.

Picture a speakeasy run by prepubescent boys. It was here, among beat-up couches, boomboxes, and Mountain Dew cans, that we would wait for our moment to caddy. In between the caddymaster calling out our last names, we would play cards and basketball—betting any quarters or snacks we had on hand. As a result of this child gambling ring, and the fact that some days my name was never called to caddy, this gig occasionally *cost* me money.

You heard that right. Some days, I would leave a full day's shift having never gotten to caddy at all—pedaling my bike, pockets empty, having just spent six hours in a windowless shack.

Recounting this experience at the dinner table, my parents were understandably a little horrified. "You must have been so bored!" they'd cry.

It's a reasonable conclusion. But actually, Mom and Dad? It was the exact opposite. Those years of getting up early, waiting impatiently, playing cards, eating chuckwagons, and what on the surface looked like nothing were actually some of the most entertaining times of my life . . . to this day!

The Boredom Myth

Kind of like sushi is a gift to our palate, boredom is a gift to our soul. Also like sushi, boredom is sometimes wrapped in what, on the surface, seems like really nasty seaweed. But then we power through it anyway and are like . . . good call, bro.

—Joe Beckman

I wrote the above Deep Thought® at 6:17 a.m. during a recent writing session. I had every intention of editing it out. However, like boredom, the sentiment is kind of growing on me.

When you see the word boredom (perhaps in this header, or my quote, or this introductory paragraph . . . are you bored of this term yet?), you might think of:

- Traffic jams (with no fun songs on the radio)

- DMVs on a bad day (or a good day)

- A five-year-old's dance recital (sorry Sophia, but those were excruciating)

When we evaluate our days, we're drawn to busyness

and dismiss dull moments that feel like a poor use of our ever-fleeting time. In our go-go-go society, deeming something to be a "waste of our time" is one of the harshest insults we have.

This culture of fearing boredom is only intensified by weirdo motivational speakers (ahem) who love to shout things like . . .

- You only get one shot!

- Make every moment matter!

- You are the author of your story!

With thoughts like these, who would want to waste a single moment in traffic? Who would want to leave even a single page of their story blank?

So . . . like avoiding a cold shower, we do everything we possibly can to avoid boredom. Stepping into it, even for a short period of time, can feel almost painful.

How do I know?

"I know! Because you like cold showers?"

No! It's because I am the *king* of avoiding boredom.

Ask anyone! (But maybe leave that random person at the grocery store alone this time.) If you've spent time with me, you know first-hand that there is no one who feels the pain of boredom more than me.

Naps feel like a trap. Sitting still, standing by, or hanging out are all hard things for me and my brain. I look for anything and everything I can to prevent boredom from appearing in my life. I even tricked myself into liking infomercials!

However, as I've been reflecting back on my life and my journey toward legacy, I can't help but think that I've been way *off* by trying to always be so *on*.

The Boredom Epidemic

I did a little research around the state of boredom in America and, let me assure you, these revelations are anything but boring.

Let's start with the basics. Boredom is defined as:

The state of feeling disinterested in one's surroundings, having nothing to do, or feeling that life is dull.

Disinterested.
Nothing.
Dull.

The state of boredom seems pretty universally grim, but it actually exists on a continuum that stretches out pretty long! Most of us feel it in a temporary state (called *transient boredom*). Some, however, feel it more permanently. Chronic boredom is known to cause higher levels of loneliness, academic failure, and self-destructive behaviors.

For our purposes, we'll focus on the majority of people who experience transient boredom, specifically within the US.

A new study of two thousand American adults and their perspectives found that . . .

- 60 percent of adults believe their life is too "grown-up."

- 73 percent miss aspects of their childhood, like time with friends (50 percent), less responsibilities (52 percent), or birthday parties (25 percent).

- You'll notice that no one mentioned missing one-of-a-kind rocks from the woods. Again, maybe not my best idea.

- We spend over *one-third* of our waking hours (the equivalent of eighty-seven days a year!) feeling *disinterested . . . nothing . . . dull . . .*

BORED!

No wonder we're all feeling tired, depressed, and down. We're bored out of our minds! And if you're spending a third of your time fighting that nothingness, you're going to be exhausted.

But I want you to think about it this way . . .

Imagine I told you that over the next twelve months, you were going to get punched in the face eighty-seven times.

You won't know when, or where, or what days, or even who will deliver the punches. Unfortunately, though, in the next year, you'll average about seven face punches a month.

First, you would most likely not want to be my friend

much longer. Second, if you accepted that I was telling the truth, you would be faced with two options.

Option 1: Do everything you can to avoid the punch.

Option 2: Suck it up and start preparing for the inevitable. Maybe get a hockey mask.

In my experience, option 1 is what too many of us choose . . . but I already *told you* these face punches are unavoidable!

We put a ton of energy into avoiding boredom, even though we know it's coming. Then, when it inevitably (but predictably) does come, our instinct is to simply complain about it. We act surprised and betrayed, feeling purely unlucky that our lives are so boring.

Friends, the punches are coming! Boredom is here! (I mean, hopefully not *literally* here in this moment while you are reading this book.) But it's been training for months, and it's ready to unload some jabs, crosses, and uppercuts to you, me, and everyone!

Fortunately, it's not all bad news. It may be hard to

see this when the punches are coming, but we are *better* because of boredom.

Think about it . . . some of your best, most creative ideas, dreams, adventures, and friendships may have been forged in the fiery misery of boredom. You were stuck. You had nothing to do. And so the only other thing to do was connect with something in yourself or someone around you. And you did.

Look around. Some of your most prized possessions might be in your possession solely as a cure for boredom!

I'm looking at the Cactus Canyon Pinball Machine that I "mid-life-crisis" purchased three months back. Why do you think I purchased it?

Because it gives the room a pop of color? No.
Because you have the maturity level of a ten-year old? No. (I mean yes/no on this one.)
Because you like cold showers? No! Stop asking me that!

Because your basement was kind of bland, and you really like going down to your basement because as much as you love your wife and children, every once in a while, you need a little "me" time?

Wow. That's pretty good, but not quite there . . .

Because you've always felt the opposite of bored when you've played pinball?

Nailed it.

In Defense of Boredom

Have you ever declared that you were simply *bored to death*?

Every day, we put our buddy boredom on trial for ruining days, wasting time, and, apparently, ending lives. In the interest of fairness, let's play that trial out.

We're not headed to the courtroom, though. We're going back to the caddyshack.

All those years ago, my parents were quick to brand my summer as "boring." My day started out with early-morning infomercials and sometimes passed

with no work in a windowless room. On the surface, they seem obviously correct. Boredom should be *doing time* for wasting my time!

In the court of law, boredom might be facing three charges: causing a young Joe Beckman to feel disinterested, nothing, and dull. In the caddyshack, though, boredom proved to be a healing force and an essential part of my legacy.

That summer, I learned the secret power of boredom. The lazy mornings and long afternoons proved boredom could be a source of rest and rejuvenation, allowing me to build up my reserves for when the next big moment arrived.

I may have been waking up early to see those infomercials, but watching them also proved to be a restful activity (at least compared to the flashiness of cartoons). By giving my brain the space to wander, sparks appeared!

(And no, I'm not just talking about sparks that may have resulted from Master Ron's dubious beef jerky machine.)

In watching the enthusiasm of these featured inventors, I was inspired to come up with my own businesses and ways to make money. Something that on the surface seemed like a boring, mindless activity was actually paving the way toward the caddyshack, and ultimately *everything* we have done and will continue to do with TILL360.

Within those windowless walls, my imagination truly took hold. Alongside my fellow caddying hopefuls, I invented games (and creative ways to lose my money before I had even earned it).

While it would've been nice to have a cellphone at that time to record the grand championship of an original sport we called Shaftball, I'm grateful that I had those summers free of distraction. Now, flashy images, audio, and endless stories aren't limited to Saturday mornings. We're quick to pull out devices to fend off the slightest sense of emptiness every time it creeps in.

Be honest—have you ever pulled out your phone in an effort to *appear* busy? Perhaps you've been in line at the coffee shop or waiting to meet up with a friend. There have been moments I've convinced myself that if I don't hop on my own phone, the people on phones around me will start texting things like . . .

- *At sbux. Guy here who looks like he's letting his mind wander LOL*

- *This weird, backward-hat hippie guy in front of me in line must have NOTHING going on in his life*

- *I have a gut instinct that this phoneless man is so inspirational*

Okay, I wouldn't mind that last one.

We're so afraid of boredom that we fight against even *appearing* like we might be experiencing it.

I might be the first to say that I don't do well with boredom. But I also know now, as an adult, that I don't do well with no rest. Embracing the rejuvenation and sparks of ideas that may accompany boredom allows me to navigate these slower periods of life without beating myself up.

There's no such thing as wasted time! There's only rest, rejuvenation, and replenishment of your reserves.

Okay . . . I lied. Not about the myth of wasted time! But about those three concepts being the *only* Rs.

There's also Robbie Robinson.

What Boredom Sounds Like

People connect to your energy, not your talent.
Sing with energy and sing with care.

—Robbie Robinson

(ish. It's hard to transcribe exact quotes when you're in the presence of greatness)

I was a senior in high school when I had a super unique realization that no other teenager has ever thought before.

I was *sick* of school.

I was sick of endless tests and lectures. I was sick of squeaky chairs and dull pencils and the same hallways I had walked for years.

I was bored.

By that time, I had already spent over a decade as a student. I didn't think that one more year spent sitting in the classroom would contribute to my legacy. I was ready to get out there! Wasn't this wasted time, preventing me from entering the real world and applying what I was learning?

I realized eventually that I was facing two choices.

Option 1: Accept that high school is inevitably boring, keep my head down, and get through the end by doing the bare minimum.

Option 2: Embrace the boredom! Understand that the things I do in school may not feel immediately relevant to my legacy or long-term goals, but they could prove useful in other ways.

To a bored, high-school me, neither of these options felt great. Option 1 sounded miserable, and option 2 sounded sketchy at best. But at least there was no face-punching involved.

Right around the time I resolved to make the most of my boring senior year, an opportunity arrived in the form of Robbie Robinson.

Robbie Robinson was one of the greatest gospel singers of our time . . . and he was coming to our school. He was offering to do a concert, sales from which would benefit our school and make us a ton of money.

There was only one catch: he needed back-up. Robbie loved incorporating the student choir into his school performances, and our administration eagerly agreed. What they didn't tell Robbie was . . .

We didn't actually have a student choir.

Recruitment quickly began in anticipation of his arrival. When things got desperate, they turned to the theater kids. After all, we at least had experience being on stage.

I had joined theater after an injury took me out of sports. Now, I'd be joining choir because my (ahem, Catholic military) school administration's white lie was at risk of angering the best baritone in Minnesota.

This feels like a weird origin story. It wasn't really in line with my existing interests. It wouldn't be the start of my singing journey or an opportunity to get discovered. But it was something.

Little did I know, it would be a spark.

Choir rehearsals began and I quickly proved to be a stand-out . . . in all the worst ways. In between verses of gospel hits, I noticed a pattern emerging. When I sang my heart out, Robbie had a tendency to glance at my section with a horrified look on his face. When I masterfully lip-synced, he praised our group's talents.

Note taken. I would coast in the back of the choir. I had grown used to just waiting out boring school moments that didn't serve my interests.

The night of the big performance, the attendance was massive. Hundreds of people poured into the auditorium—a sold-out crowd! Before the first song had ended, everyone was on their feet and dancing. The energy continued for the rest of the show.

Finally, we reached the grand finale: "This Little Light of Mine." A crowd favorite, Robbie began doing endless reprises of the famous chorus. He also used the song as an opportunity to call out soloists.

I smiled and lip synced proudly as my friends—who

were really there for the singing—got their moments at the mic. Robbie clearly had singing and scouting chops, as he successfully highlighted the classmates who I considered the best singers.

Emily sang that she would let her little light shine.

Justin declared that he would not hide his light under a bushel.

Robbie . . . was looking at me.

I felt my legs go numb from fear—not from boredom!—as Robbie Robinson turned to the crowd. "I think we have time for one more soloist."

Now I was doing a frantic reprise of my own: *Not me, not me, not me, please not me.*

"Joe. Come on down."

I felt like one of the cartoon characters from my Saturday morning shows. As I walked slowly to the microphone, I thought I could hear a record scratch and a voiceover start to play:

Yep, that's me. I bet you're wondering how I got into this mess . . .

Nearing the mic, I had to make a split-second decision. I had already spent my rehearsals lip-syncing. I had resigned myself to a position in the back of the choir. I had yet to make meaning from this slow, song-filled time in my life.

Was this my moment?

Before I knew it, I was leading the crowd in an out-of-tune, oddly paced, and brazenly loud version of "This Little Light of Mine." The classic verse had never felt longer. But when it was over . . .

I got a standing ovation.

(Okay, yes, if you've been paying attention, you may remember that the crowd was already on their feet to dance. But they didn't sit down!)

If the clapping wasn't affirming enough, Robbie Robinson pulled me aside after the show. "Joe," he said. "You have a gift."

"Umm . . . I'm not that good of a singer . . ." I said, confused about where he was going with this.

"I'm not talking about your singing." Cool. We're on the same page. "I'm talking about your energy. You have the energy that could change lives."

Something clicked for me in that moment. Robbie Robinson had come to my school to sing, but it was his conversation with me after that really moved me. During this time of immense boredom, when it felt like I was making no progress toward my goal, Robbie reminded me: something was still stirring. In small, everyday moments—even those that felt slow—I was fostering the sparks I would need for the next stage of my legacy.

When the time was right, those sparks would be ready to shine.

Letting Your Boredom Shine

I often think back to my first conversation with Curtis Slater, when I almost had to push him into the river. What he pointed out that day was my boredom. I had been doing the same thing over and over, allowing my work to become stagnant. I wasn't *fighting* the boredom, but I certainly wasn't embracing it either.

When Curtis called out my boredom, my first instinct was to be defensive. I was more willing to calculate my odds of overpowering him in our pontoon boat than to simply consider how this slower period in my life could fuel the next chapter of my legacy.

We're too quick to dismiss boredom as a hindrance—a passive roadblock on the way to our true mission. When we embrace boredom, we see it for what it truly is.

The best kind of boredom calls us out . . . whether from the choir or from our own complacency.

It's an invitation!

Dear Joe,

It seems like things are kinda slow for building your legacy right now. That's ok—you don't need to resort to peddling rocks to your neighbors.

Why not use this time to reflect and to dig into the things that your busy brain pushes to the side? Let your mind wander. Give yourself the freedom to rest. Seriously, put down the rocks.

Social media companies are making billions to distract you from boredom and occupy your brain space. That should clue you in that these things have value! They're an essential part of your legacy.

Your friend,

Snu Z. Fest

Caveman Wisdoms: Legacy Edition

One day, when my daughter Sophia was just a baby, I had her out for a walk in the stroller. I wanted to take advantage of an unseasonably warm late fall Minnesota day, and the fresh air would be good for both of us, right? Plus, the dog needed to be walked, and I could do that while I pushed the stroller.

And I needed to make a work call. No big deal. I can talk while I walk! This was a win-win-win.

Except it wasn't. My attention was pulled in multiple directions . . . I was simply juggling a bunch of responsibilities while being outside.

Yes, I was technically breathing in fresh air, which was one of my goals that day. But I had a startling moment of clarity while all of this was happening: I was outside, but I was definitely not fully benefiting from being outside. I couldn't hear leaves rustling or birds chirping, or Sophia babbling, or my feet hitting the pavement.

Did I think just walking with the stroller would be boring?
Not the best use of my time?
I'm not sure, but I did know that I got it all wrong.

We all need some time to just be. Solitude, or the ability to be on your own, is not the same as boredom and loneliness. Solitude is the time your brain needs to just be quiet and really know yourself.

Dr. Vivek Murthy, the current US Surgeon General, talks about the need to cultivate solitude as one component for combatting our national loneliness crisis. Yes, you read that right . . . learning how to be alone with your thoughts could actually be one way to bolster connection with others. When you know yourself and are comfortable with who you are, you're more genuine when you connect with others at work, in your family, or in other social settings.

So, what does this look like?

Well, when you're on a walk, just be on a walk! Even if it's not every time you're outside, be intentional about taking one walk per week without

your Airpods in with
a podcast or audiobook or music on
distracting you from just being alone with your thoughts.

If walking isn't your thing, maybe meditating could be. When you're just starting out, the goal is a very short time of silent, deep thought without distractions. It's so much harder than you think!

When you first start, make your goal thirty seconds. Then build up to a minute, then two. Be aware of how you feel after you do this, and recognize how different it feels than being bored.

CHAPTER FOUR

Meet Your (Inner) Maker

When I was a kid, I was thrown into America's largest prison.

Okay, maybe not "thrown." More like "firmly escorted to."

And did I say "America's largest prison"?

I meant America's largest *mall*'s only prison.

The Mall of America is as "Minnesota" as the state fair and lakes. As a kid, it felt like Midwestern Disneyland—complete with the sugary food, endless shopping, and rides!

It's any kid's ultimate playground, with nearly three million square feet of retail space and endless opportunities to get in trouble.

For good reason, the Mall of America has a large security force, designed to keep rebellious kids like me in line.

You've heard of *Paul Blart: Mall Cop*. But have you heard of *Mall Cops: Mall of America*?

It's a real thing! TLC once made a one-hour special following the security team at the MOA. The show was so popular that it was turned into a twelve-episode series.

This was back in 2010, but let's just say, if *Mall Cops* was filming back when Clint and I were young shoppers, they would've needed at least thirteen episodes.

When you hear that I was detained at the Mall of America, you can probably guess my crime immediately. After all, the world-famous shopping center has over five hundred different stores to choose from!

I can hear you now: "Which store did you shoplift from, Joe? Did you hold up Auntie Anne's? Did you misread the toy store sign and think it said 'Burglar-A-Bear Workshop'?"

Listen, I may be a criminal, but I'm not cliché.

No, Clint and I took part in a crime that was something much *colder*: fishing ice from our food-court sodas and dropping said cubes from the mall's towering third-story balcony.

It felt like harmless hijinks. Ice never feels like it'll do that much damage and, worst case scenario, the evidence will melt before we get caught!

Unfortunately, while the third-floor balcony gave us a great view of our targets, it also gave them a great view of us. It wasn't long before we heard the beeping and clicking of walkie-talkies and the mall cops closing in.

We were escorted down to the security office and quickly found ourselves surrounded by hardened criminals—people who had stolen, or kidnapped . . . or budged in line at Camp Snoopy.

We tried to look tough, as in if any of them were to give us even the slightest bit of attitude, we would mess them up. You don't want to mess with this Mama Bear.

So when a cop holding a cup of coffee that was likely about as bland as his tone of voice blurted out,

"Joe Beckman? Clint Jamison? Are you Joe and Clint?"

I kept my badass demeanor. "Sup?"

He looked again at the report in his other hand, and in front of the entire room said,

"Looks like we have ourselves some real winners in our midst. You mind telling everyone what you're down here for?"

I looked around. Every burglar/offender/murderer (okay, that's a stretch) in that room was there because they *truly* committed *real* crimes, and they were staring at me.

"I . . . we . . . ahhh . . . propelled objects off the fourth floor onto unsuspecting victims below us."

"And by objects he means small chunks of ice."

You could practically hear the eyerolls from the more hardened criminals in the room.

Our consequence was that we were not to step foot inside the MOA for twelve months.

"Your pictures are going to be on this wall, and every day, my security team looks at these pictures. They see you in here again in the next year, you'll be making closer friendships with many of those boys out there."

Our Brains Are Amazing

When I look back at the choice Clint and I made that day, I think what all adults who have adult brains think . . .

Why on earth would you have made such a stupid choice?
Which in turn got me thinking . . .
How many other times did I make a choice that I got wrong?
Which in turn got me thinking . . .
How many other choices have I made that I got right?
Which of course got me thinking . . .
How many freaking choices do we make every day?

With my laptop up, and my Internet at full strength, I went to the almighty Google and asked: "on average, how many choices does a human being make every day?"

Google delivered a fascinating response.

Little kids—like toddler kids—make, get this, 3,000 individual choices every day.

And adults, with a bit more responsibility on our plates, are at roughly 35,000 choices every day.

Where did that put Clint and me, teenagers on the top floor at the Mall of America? Right in the middle. Probably 16,000 choices every day.

Now don't get me wrong, *most* of these everyday choices are benign and not worthy of critical thought. They are small decisions that play rather insignificant roles in the whole scheme of things.

However, there are always some within the 3,000 or 16,000 or 35,000 choices that add up a little differently. Choices that don't just impact us, but also impact others.

Think about the kid in the cafeteria who trips and spills their tray, and everyone starts laughing. In that moment, you have a choice.

Somebody says, "I got this great new way of making some extra money, and sure, it's not exactly ethical, and I don't believe in the product, but hey, it's money." In that moment, you have a choice.

Don't even get me started with the landmines of choices we have every day on social media.

However, I'll say this much. Before you hit "send" on the message disparaging someone else, or before you click "post" on that picture you will regret . . .

You have a choice. And you have control over it.

I meet a lot of students who say things like . . .

I want to be remembered as a good person.
I want to be remembered as a great friend.
I want to be remembered as a great leader.

And to want it is awesome. But unfortunately, we're

not remembered by what we *want*, we're remembered ultimately by what we do.

How we talk to people.
How we treat people.
The choices we make when everyone's watching and the ones we make when no one is watching.

Another way to say it is that our legacies tomorrow will be defined by our actions today. This chapter is a look into that.

And good news! When it comes to stories about choices like the one Clint and I made at the MOA that day, I have a treasure trove to choose from.

As a first foray into felonious activity, "ice dropping" was a relatively tame crime and scene. Our next scheme, however, would unfortunately involve something much more sinister.

Trouble in Whoville

I may have related to *A Christmas Story*'s Flick, but one December, I embodied a very different holiday icon: *the Grinch*.

In a misguided attempt at teenage rebellion, Clint and I decided to steal Christmas.

In hindsight, an alternate title to this book could be, *Just Stop Hanging Out with Clint.*

I also maybe should've steered clear of Christmas movies and the emotional turmoil they seemed to stir within me.

If you've never heard of "Grinching," the concept is exactly what it sounds like. You and your buddy sneak through neighborhoods in the dark, stealing Christmas decorations that have been placed outside of homes. Anything—and everything—goes, from lights to lawn ornaments and blow-up reindeer.

I could blame this activity on the fact that I grew up in a small town, with nothing else to do, or that I had some long-standing feud with plastic holiday decor.

It wasn't me! It was the manger-anger!

In reality, the largest appeal of the activity was that it was something to do, and I wasn't at an age where

I automatically thought about the consequences of my actions.

You know those crazy years—where you simultaneously think you're the most important person in the world *and* that nothing you do matters. It's a confusing dichotomy that becomes easier to ignore if you're busy stealing elves with your best friend.

One night, the target of our "bah humbug" burglary was the house of a former friend by the name of Troy Rhein. Troy was someone we used to hang out with from elementary school. As we grew older and formed more distinct friend groups within the strict social hierarchy of school (more on that later), we drifted apart.

There wasn't any particular event that caused the end of the friendship, though.

That is, until his dad caught me and Clint stealing plastic candy canes from his front yard.

Pros of going for the candy canes: relatively light, highly portable. Can even be used for walking assistance if you sustain an injury during the great escape.

Cons of going for the candy canes: real candy canes naturally sharpen into a point as you eat them and could be used for self-defense; plastic candy canes are just a really embarrassing thing to be clutching as you're reprimanded by a former friend's father.

"What are you doing?" he asked the two of us as we stood ashamedly on his porch.

As it turns out, the only thing more embarrassing than getting caught stealing candy canes is trying to come up with an explanation for why.

In that simple question, I could hear a million other questions. It was evident that the exhaustion in his voice didn't just come from the late hour it was—he was baffled and dismayed.

I was good friends with his kid! I had sat at their kitchen table!

"What are you doing?" has to be one of the worst questions you can be asked as a rebellious kid. It comes with a sense of doom. Even though the asker seems like they don't know what's going on, the jig is up.

You've been caught.

The only worse question comes from your parents, later: "What were you thinking?"

This question is hard because there's only one right answer, and it stings to admit: "I wasn't."

Difference Makers, Takers, and Fakers

Too often, we don't consider the little moments to be a part of our legacy.

We incorrectly think that in order to leave a positive impact in someone's life, we have to do something big like rescue a person from a burning car in the nick of time or donate millions of dollars to a country in need.

Or conversely, we think if anyone is going to remember us for a negative impact we made, surely it has to be something so bad that we remember it and still shudder in shame to this day.

But I assure you, the roads, good or bad, that we are building for others to walk on behind us are not just being forged by the big moments. While they certainly play a role, it's truly

the small things,
the tiny daily (up to 35,000) choices we make,
that add up over time

and surround those big, life-changing moments

that define how we will be remembered.

We can allow ourselves to have bad days, or to be stupid kids, or to "live while we're young." We tell ourselves that it's never too late to change and that tomorrow is always a fresh start.

In a lot of ways, these sentiments are true. When used in retrospect, they can even be helpful. We shouldn't define ourselves by our worst moments.

However, we also shouldn't think that our definition is only crafted in the best environments,

or when we reach the perfect age,
or when we obtain the dreamiest job,
or when we reach "quesadilla-maker-worthy" levels in our savings accounts.

The roads we are building are a mix of everything we've ever done, everything we are currently doing, and everything we will do! Even if you hate this whole idea and would prefer your legacy simply disappear like a puff of smoke, it can't. Your legacy is being forged whether you like it or not.

And make no mistake about it: while we're working on our own legacies, not only are we playing a role in the legacy of others, but they are 100 percent playing a role in ours.

Yes . . . keep your eyes forward, focused on the road that you're charting for yourself. But don't lose sight of the fact that behind you are millions of tiny strings connecting you to other people.

You have a choice in the role you play.

And the really cool thing about this is it takes so little.

A small smile
A short conversation
A quick connection

The way I say it when I'm speaking to students is,

"It's not about changing the world . . . it's about changing one person's day."

We've already talked about the positive impacts of Undercover Angels—those unsuspecting people whose moments of kindness remain a light in your life, long after an interaction has ended.

Undercover Angels appear at unexpected moments—whether you're encountering one or becoming one! At other times, though, we have a clear opportunity to make an impact on someone else's legacy and life. In these moments, we have three clear choices.

You can be a
Difference Maker,
Difference Taker, or
Difference Faker.

These three identities show up in the critical moments. Sometime between your best friend saying, "What if . . ." and grabbing the candy canes, you choose which role to embody.

The Difference Maker knows when to speak up, becoming a force for good or a barrier against evil.

The Difference Taker finds joy in bringing others down. In snuffing out someone's light. (*In the case of Grinching, literally snuffing out the light.*)

The Difference Faker is the bystander, who dismisses their guilt on technicalities. As long as it wasn't your idea or your direct actions causing the harm, it's not *really* your fault.

I tend to tell students that the breakdown for making, taking, and faking is as follows:

Ten percent of the time we're Makers: actively making the difference.

Ten percent of the time we're Takers: making the bad choice—taking away from someone else's legacy in a poor attempt to add excitement to ours.

Eighty percent of the time we're Fakers: we're in the background, passive observers of the choices of others.

My guess is that if I gave you thirty seconds to reflect on your childhood, you would be able to easily do two things . . .

Identify people from your past that fit into these definitions.

Identify times when *you* have been these definitions yourself.

And although you would think those rare moments of being the star or the villain would stick the longest, I've found that it's the critical moments of inaction, being a Difference Faker, that haunt me the most.

A Faker in the Making

I went to a military high school. In an effort to reinforce good behavior, we could receive "promotions" and new titles for clean uniforms, academic success, or a host of other reasons. For some people in my school, moving up this military chain of command was the single most important thing.

Of course, this was still a high school—so one stressful hierarchy wasn't enough. We also had your typical unspoken, but readily enforced, human hierarchy . . . I call it the social chain of command. You know the kind. Somewhere around middle school, we lose our readiness to love and accept everyone. To bury our own insecurities, we begin shoving each other down and climbing the ranks.

For some people in my school, myself included, moving up the social chain of chain of command was the single most important thing. They would do whatever it took to move up, even if it meant pushing others down (sometimes literally) in the process.

A boy who I'll call Shane was at the very bottom of my class's social chain of command. If we're being honest, he may have been at the very bottom of the whole school.

It's hard to ever fully identify why kids can decide to be so cruel. One of the primary things that classmates used to tease Shane, however, was his reaction to stress.

When Shane was overwhelmed, the muscles in his face and neck would tense up, creating an unusual appearance that other kids loved to make fun of and provoke.

If Shane was being teased, the tensing would start.

And once the tensing started, the teasing only got worse.

I had one class with Shane—World History. I can still picture the classroom and the way it seemed to subtly reinforce the social groupings we had invented for ourselves.

I sat in the front, a beloved position for its proximity to the door and the lectern.

What can I say—I've always been a speaker.

I was joined in the front row by my friend Kyle. Kyle was the top of the social hierarchy, and I'd be lying if I said our friendship wasn't a little bit strategic. He was athletic and funny, often at the expense of others. Sitting near him meant that, while soaking up history lessons, I'd also achieve some extra coolness through osmosis . . . or something like that.

Look, this isn't a story about science class.

Bonding with Kyle in world history was also a good way to avoid his ire. Proximity to the cool kids allowed them to either pull you up the ranks, or shove you down. So far, so good.

Shane, however, had a different experience with kids like Kyle. Understandably, he steered clear of us—sitting all the way in the back. I have to imagine that he took solace in the space away from the prying eyes of his peers, all hoping to catch him in a moment of stress.

He sat quietly at his desk all semester, mainly avoiding attention and the wrath that only high schoolers can bring. The end of the year, however, brought a new challenge—this time from our teacher.

The final project, which would determine a substantial portion of our final grade, was to be a presentation. We could talk about anything, as long as we tied it back to a topic from class.

For me, the prospect was exciting. I'd always been fairly comfortable in front of a crowd, and I knew that my buddies in class would be ready to laugh and clap at all my cues.

Even for the kids that didn't like public speaking,

though, the idea of individual presentations was exciting for a different reason.

There was a tense curiosity about how the project would go for Shane.

When the big day arrived, a nervous energy filled the room. I'd like to think that many of us were anxiously hoping that he would get through it okay. In reality, it felt as though his suffering was going to serve as a reprieve from an otherwise boring school day.

Shane slowly walked to the front of the classroom with a box. As he queued up the presentation, the day's topic and the contents of his box were revealed: WWII fighter planes. He had brought a dozen perfectly crafted model planes, which we soon found out he had built himself.

At the beginning of the presentation, his voice was soft. Even from the front row, I had a hard time understanding him. As he continued, though, his confidence grew. With each model he held up and explained, his expertise and passion for the topic grew clearer.

He had even picked out a relevant video clip to play.

(If you ever want to win over a group of high schoolers, don't underestimate the power of breaking up class with a video.)

In the glow of the screen, I saw Shane crack a tentative smile.

As we walked out of class, it felt as though something had shifted. Shane had done a good job with his presentation, and he carried himself with just a bit more confidence.

Unfortunately, the biggest fear of those in power is someone else taking it away.

Kyle and another friend were waiting right outside the classroom doorway as Shane packed up his planes. Unwilling to let Shane enjoy the glory of his successful presentation for too long, Kyle hatched a plan.

Right as Shane walked out of the class, Kyle shoved his friend. The sidekick went careening into Shane, knocking him against the doorframe and sending his box of planes flying.

At that point, Kyle had given himself plausible deniability. He could pretend it was just an accident, just the jostling of a high school hallway.

"Oops, sorry man," he said with a little grin, holding his hands in the air.

As he walked away, though, and saw the planes scattered around the floor . . . he couldn't resist taking things one step further.

He approached a plane that Shane had so proudly held up just ten minutes earlier, a plane for which we now knew the name and history and strength.

And he lifted his foot.

And he crushed it.

And we all watched, stunned, as Shane picked up the pieces.

And no one said a word.

I still get a pit in my stomach thinking about that day with Kyle and Shane. Kyle was no doubt a Difference Taker, and at the time I walked away and felt good that I hadn't been the one to stomp on the plane.

Now, however, I see it differently. I wasn't necessarily a Difference Taker, but I most certainly was a Difference Faker. In a moment of truth, when I had the ability to add a little bit of light, I chose to stay silent. By doing so, I added to the dark.

I think about what my silence meant *for* Shane, and what my continued friendship with Kyle meant *about* me.

It was like I wanted to be remembered as a Difference Maker, by stopping all of the Difference Takers, but I would freeze and become a Difference Faker.

Fortunately, we're not defined by our worst moments. And fortunately, around senior year, following an empowering speech about airing out our grievances and reconciling before graduation, a lot of us apologized to Shane.

But I started to feel guilty about that day long before senior year.

Why didn't I say something earlier, when it would have mattered more? Why do we wait?

Everything in my heart screamed, "Do something! Say something! Go up to Shane and tell him he did a great job. Tell Kyle to knock it off! Go up to a teacher and report it."

And I did nothing. Not because I wasn't good. I was good. I think I just needed one person to convince me that I could be great.

Maybe that's why you're reading this book. Because for so long, you've been so close to leaving a positive impact on others that is impossible to forget. Maybe you're just looking for the courage.

Here . . . I'm giving it to you.

We need you.
Your family needs you.
Our world needs you.

So please . . . take it.

A Midfield Miracle

If you thought my military high school was intense, you should've seen my elementary school.

In fifth grade, I was playing in the Super Bowl *every single day*.

At least, that's what it felt like. When you're young and competitive and only given one precious hour of recess per day, every second of flag football on the playground counts.

I was proud to routinely serve as a team captain and quarterback. At the beginning of every outdoor break, while other kids meandered to the swings or lined up for the slide, me and one other kid would start picking our teams, rapid-fire.

Every recess, we'd take turns—calling out the names of our closest friends, our fastest allies, and our strongest peers.

Every recess, we'd take turns—who got the first pick.

And every recess, we'd take turns . . . picking Chris Johnson last.

Chris Johnson was a nice kid, but he wasn't the strongest football player. Playground rules dictated that he had to be included, but it wouldn't come without a little reluctance from the captains.

It sounds dramatic, but trust me! There are no higher stakes than fourth quarter in fifth grade.

One recess, the clock was winding down and our ears were straining for the end-of-recess whistle that we knew would come at any second. My team was down by one touchdown and had been slowly progressing through the midfield.

We got one last snap off, and my two best receivers started running.

It was going to be a long shot. But shouldn't Hail Marys hold more weight at a Catholic middle school?

I bobbed and weaved, looking for the perfect window to get the ball to one of my best guys. Unfortunately, the other team also knew they were my best guys. I watched in dismay as they were both quickly covered.

Shifting my gaze toward the other side, I saw Chris

standing downfield, wide open. He waved his arms, a huge smile spreading across his face.

I quickly averted my gaze.

I continued to dance around defenders, buying time until something better could open up. By this point, Chris had made it all the way to the end zone and remained completely unmarked. He waved his arms and clapped his hands for the ball.

I looked right at him . . .

And threw the ball to the opposite side. One of my receivers had finally broken free and, with a leaping catch, scored the game-winning touchdown.

The joy among my teammates was immediate. As we all headed back toward the school, there were claps on the back and whooping coming from all of us. All of us, that is, except Chris.

I found myself feeling a little annoyed.

"I don't know why he's so upset," I remarked to a friend. "He was on the winning team!"

Fortunately, even Chris's inexplicable sulkiness couldn't dampen my excitement. The only thing better than winning recess football was reliving the highlights with my siblings when I got home.

The kitchen table was my SportsCenter, and I was the star of every highlight.

This story, however, wasn't just going to be an anecdote. To me, it felt like an *audition*. My older brother, Matt, routinely played football with his friends after school. He was two years older than me and consistently told me that fifth grade was *far* too young to play with the seventh graders.

With this pinnacle victory and historic throw, I was sure my luck would change.

Matt didn't react to my jaw-dropping tale with as much enthusiasm as I was hoping. Still, when he headed out to play with his friends after dinner, he finally didn't reject my request to come along.

When we arrived at the field, I watched my recess routine play out on a larger scale. Two captains were selected and quickly began dividing up the teams. I tried not to feel disappointment at being picked last. I was, after all, much younger than the other kids. I knew that I would prove myself soon enough.

The chance to make an impression came toward the end of the game. I was wide open in the endzone! Even as the older boys towered above me, I managed to ditch my mark and stood confident in my ability to make a game-winning catch.

But the ball never came.

I watched as the quarterback's eyes skimmed right over me, opting for a tougher throw to a different receiver.

When the play ended, I stormed home.

Yes, I was smaller than the seventh graders. Yes, some of them may even have been better than me. But I was on the team! How was I supposed to get better if they never even gave me a chance with the ball?

Oh.

I didn't get a touchdown that day, but I did get an epiphany. I got an idea of how Chris was feeling every day at recess. And I hated it.

The next time recess rolled around and we all lined up for the drafting of St. Michael's Fifth Grade Super Bowl XCV, much to everyone's surprise, I picked Chris first.

I didn't throw it to him every time, but I know that I threw it to him twice. I remember the first time, he caught it . . . and the second time, he dropped it, but that didn't matter. What mattered was for the first day I could remember, Chris walked back into school with a little confidence, feeling for once as if he was part of the team.

As it turns out, a touchdown is only worth six points. Feeling seen is worth everything.

Friends, we get up to 35,000 choices every single day. That's 35,000 opportunities to shine a little bit of light into someone else's dark.

Do you remember that breakdown we talked about earlier?

Ten percent of the time we're Makers.
Ten percent of the time we're Takers.
Eighty percent of the time we're Fakers.

What if we could switch the top number with the bottom one?

What if 80 percent of the time we were actively looking for opportunities to make the choice to be a Difference Maker? What if we were seeking out moments that could really impact someone else's life or legacy?

We can give ourselves the grace to not be perfect, while at the same time challenging ourselves to be better.

And here's the best part . . . no matter where you are in your legacy, no matter how much time is left on the clock . . . you have 35,000 opportunities today to move that percentage in the right direction.

Remember . . . it's not about changing the world; it's about changing one person's day.

So if you've got some work to do, if you've fumbled a few of the choices like I have, don't stress . . . don't get down . . . don't quit . . .

It's never too late for a Hail Mary.

Caveman Wisdoms: Legacy Edition

No matter where you're living right now—with your parents, in a dorm room, in your first apartment, or in your dream house—commit to being a Difference Maker right where you are, in whatever neighborhood you live.

Why? Because when you do, you become invested, even in small ways, and your life will be richer and better for it.

And how am I suggesting you do this? Well, that part depends on you. As mentioned earlier, you don't always have to be doing big, grand gestures as you build your legacy. You don't have to host the whole neighborhood for a cookout or buy treats from the ice cream truck for all the kids in your apartment complex. You don't need to run for subdivision trustee . . . unless settling fence disputes between neighbors is your idea of a good time. Then, by all means, go for it.

But you could take an extra minute when getting out of your car after work to say hello to the person next door. You could ask the guy across the hall in your dorm to join you for dinner. When you bake cookies or cinnamon rolls, bring a few to someone living nearby. Be the one to welcome the new people who just moved in down the street.

Already lived in your house for ten years, and feeling more like a Difference Faker? It's not too late . . . it's never too late. You can still do these things too!

Doing a small kindness likely will not have earth-shattering results that you see in the moment, but they could—what if your future best friend or spouse is right next door? What if your older neighbor could really just use someone to talk to, and that someone could be you?

When you choose to be the kind of person who invests just a bit of themselves wherever they are, those little things add up over a lifetime, and they shift that 10 percent / 10 percent / 80 percent calculation.

You never know what life will bring. It's helpful to be familiar with or even friends with people around you so that when you need a cup of sugar or you get a phone call that changes everything, there's someone there for you.

My suggestion here is simple: pick one thing to do, pick a time to do it, and make it happen. It will not only delight your neighbor, it will add value to your life.

Reflect on how it felt to do that thing. Commit to doing something again the following week. Lather, rinse, repeat.

CHAPTER FIVE

Take Stock

Earlier in the book, I highlighted my love for Saturday and its grocery store samples. It wouldn't be fair, though, to let my *second* favorite day of the week go unacknowledged: Wednesday.

On Wednesday nights, my father, Mark Beckman—captain of the fire department, expertly permed, A+ suburban dad—played for the St. Michael's Fighting Irish church league slow-pitch softball team.

These guys were excellent. They had Speedy Rick, who turned every single into a double, and Smoky Bob, who could turn double plays in the middle infield while smoking a cigarette at the same time.

There was also Bernie, a 5'3" pitcher whose only kryptonite was his belly occasionally getting in the way of his perfect moon-ball strikes.

Mark Beckman, though, was a utility player. Some

nights he played shortstop when the regular guy wasn't there. Some nights he'd play a "middle fielder"—just beyond second base in the short outfield. He was the quintessential pinch hitter . . . literally!

After the last out, the team would go to the sponsoring bar called the Commercial Club. This place was a gem! And by gem, I mean one errant cigarette butt away from the whole place going up in flames. Given that you were still allowed to smoke in the establishment (and Smoky Bob often had reason to celebrate post-game), it's a miracle we escaped unscathed.

Nearly every player on the team had a kid that was basically my age. After spending most of the innings running around with them in the woods near the diamond, we had worked up quite an appetite.

We all would pile into the Commercial Club's banquet room. The guys would sit at long tables, drinking beer and pulling hundreds of pull-tabs, which is, in essence, a slot machine the shape, size, and weight of a business card. The kids would be satisfied by feasting on the Wednesday night special: Juanita's tacos.

Say what you will about Taco Tuesdays, but I'll forever be loyal to Juanita Wednesdays. I have yet to eat a better taco in my life.

Everyone's Your Buddy

On the ride home from the bar to our house one night, we rolled up to a four-way stop. The car across the road arrived at the same time, hoping to turn in front of us.

My dad, ever the epitome of "Minnesota nice," waved him across.

Tired from a long day, and half comatose from my weekly dose of tacos, I wondered why my dad was wasting time by trying to make friends. "Why'd you wave at that guy?"

He looked at me and said,

"Because he's my buddy, Joey."

I considered the possibility that my dad actually had recognized a friend in the dark . . . but quickly deduced that he must be lying. "You do that to everyone," I protested. "Why do you always say 'hi,' or wave, or smile at people you don't even know?"

"Because *everyone's* your buddy," he said simply.

"Everyone?"

"They *could* be!" he said. "And if you assume they are, there's a better chance they will be."

Mark Beckman was so many things for me and my family growing up. One thing he was not, however, was a philosopher. In fact, whenever he would truly try to prove a point, he would usually just resort to quoting something that someone else had already said.

I'm convinced part of growing up is eventually watching your parents' favorite movies and realizing that your dad was never as clever as you thought.

Unless, of course, Hollywood was stealing these lines from him. In which case, to the writers of The *Breakfast Club*, I have just one thing to say:

"You mess with the bull, you're going to get the horns!"

Regardless, I have yet to find the film where "everyone's your buddy" could have originated. If you happen to know of one and want to officially ruin my childhood, feel free to reach out.

For now, though, my dad will be credited with that life-changing advice.

At that insignificant stop sign, after an insignificant game, he shared one of the most significant pieces of wisdom.

A wisdom that

has widened my circle,
opened more doors, and
is based on love, acceptance, cooperation, and compromise.

Everyone's your buddy.

It might sound a little elementary—and it should! My dad's wisdom that day was less of a revelation and more of a reminder. The "everyone's your buddy" mindset is reminiscent of the attitudes we all carry as children . . . and it's a lens for life that we're often too quick to relinquish.

A Lot to Unpack Here

I was tempted to make this entire chapter about retaining your childhood wonder. Working in schools has made me realize that kids, though sometimes cruel, have such a compelling capacity for wonder and kindness and forgiveness.

But a Joe Beckman that fully leaned into his childhood wonder would eat cake for breakfast every day. And would probably remain loyal to the "sounding out" method and present you with a book with a lot more typos.

The next section title has the word "malaise"! Eight-year-old Joe could never!

But wait—don't skip ahead!

That childlike curiosity almost got the best of you, huh?

The point is, we unfortunately can't stay eight years

old forever. But so many of us fail to find the middle ground—we pack away the easygoing nature of our childhoods completely in favor of maturity, and in turn, we lose many of the superpowers we once confidently owned.

You can pack away your eight-year-old self on the days you have a job interview or have to pay your taxes or are going to the DMV.

(Trust me, the only thing that can make the DMV worse is experiencing it as a child.)

But when you need compassion for a stranger, entertainment during a long drive, or enthusiasm for a tea party with your kids, you're going to want to have your little self by your side.

It's like digging around in the prop box at summer stock theater, where we put on a new show every few weeks and were constantly assigned new roles. We needed to know what pieces and costumes would best bring out our character. We needed to know when to tap into different emotions—and the more we had on hand, the better!

Similarly, when my family and I finished moving into our house and were undoing all of the packing we *just* did (don't get me started on packing again), moving through each box felt like moving through different versions of our lives. Just like in theater, we were finding out what role items could play in this new set.

Spoiler alert, though: No scene is ever improved by a homemade birdhouse. You can still throw that out.

Our range of emotions and memory bank of lessons—good and bad—work the same way. It might be tempting to throw out any trait that seems negative, or rely on the skills that have worked for you in the past.

Sometimes we fail to see that on the other side of a negative trait there is a superpower that can make our lives and the lives around us better!

And at the same time, we can *also* miss that the same is true for our positive traits.

A singular trait applied in different situations could end up being either really great or completely disastrous. The trick is knowing when to tap into the different parts of yourself.

Malaise in Malaysia

Early on in my solo speaking career, I was invited to speak in Malaysia.

This wasn't just a big deal, it was ginormous, and the pressure was intense.

All good though . . .

Pressure
Stress
Big Moments

I've dealt with all of them in my life. Generally speaking, and mostly thanks to my never-ending, always-striving intensity, I've wound up on the right side of things.

The exact intensity that got me into this glorious position was going to be what got me through it.

This felt like the culmination of everything I had been

working toward. The man who invited me managed a huge roster of in-school speakers. If I impressed him, I'd be added to his prestigious team that was constantly booking my dream gigs.

The prime minister of Malaysia was going to be there!

The weeks leading up to the conference were full of some of my most intense preparation yet. I was writing all new material and rehearsing from sun-up to sun-down. On the flight over, I had to stop myself from treating my seat neighbors to thirty-seven renditions of my thirty-minute speech.

My friends and family probably thought I was going a little crazy. But I was proud of that! This felt like my big break—I was going to make sure that I made the most of it.

On the day of the presentation, I was terrified. This speech meant everything.

And then it happened. I became so overwhelmed

with intense thoughts of screwing everything up that it became a self-fulfilling prophecy.

As I walked onto the stage, a million thoughts rushed through my head.

I can't let the person who invited me down.
I can't let myself down.
I can't let the president of Malaysia down!

Not necessarily the most helpful pep talk.

This level of high-pressure self-motivation may have driven me to land the Malaysia gig, but when I was actually walking on stage, it was the furthest thing from empowering.

My hands were shaking. My voice was shaking. And thirty seconds into the speech . . .

I forgot everything.

My mind went completely blank.

Normally, I can fumble my way through when I lose

my place. I'll ramble until I reach a transition point or a familiar start to a new story.

But this was all new material.

And I still had twenty-nine minutes and thirty seconds to go.

I'm incredibly grateful that there was no TikTok at the time, so that @ThePresidentOfMalaysia couldn't post a video of my ensuing speech, set to the sound of a trending car crash audio.

Needless to say, it was bad.

So bad that a lot of attendees didn't even pretend it wasn't bad. I didn't get any of those vague, shallow compliments that typically follow even the most mediocre of speeches. At the after party, I was met with a devastating number of those thin-lipped grimaces and quick nods.

Needless to say *again*, I took advantage of the fact that there was an after party. As did my business partner, Scott.

We had both invested a ton of time and money into this opportunity, thinking that it would quickly pay off through bookings, exposure, and partnerships. We both knew it: that dream was now over.

So yes, we may have indulged in a few adult beverages that night to power through the embarrassment. And one of us (not saying who) may have had too many beverages and said things to important people that made things a whole lot worse.

Okay, it was Scott. Sorry, buddy, I've embarrassed myself enough in this chapter. I'm not taking the fall here.

Instead of shaking hands and signing autographs, we were soon hanging our heads and packing our bags, boarding another twenty-seven-hour flight home.

This time, I was not tempted to make any speeches to my seat neighbors.

There was a part of me that was tempted to not make another speech again to anyone.

Because I put so much intense pressure on myself to

hit the game-winning home run, I froze and struck out in the bottom of the ninth.

I turned my intense focus on myself, and I hated what I saw. I wanted to completely give up the dream, start a new life, and never show my face in those crowds again.

Fortunately, at that point I had made so many mistakes, I also had the foresight to just stop listening to myself.

As I tucked my carry-on into the overhead bin, I also tucked away my intensity. It had earned me a cool opportunity, but the Malaysia trip was over.

If I couldn't shift my focus, everything else would be over too.

A Walk Down Memory Lane

I couldn't know it at the time, but Malaysia was not my big break.

Okay, no. I definitely knew once I blew it that Malaysia wasn't my big break. What I didn't know was that I would get another chance at everything I wanted.

After mourning the disastrous trip, we kept at it. And while I maybe never had a singular big break, through pursuing smaller opportunities and continuing the passion for my mission, I had a series of smaller breaks.

I kept working intensely on my material and telling stories, and audiences were smiling again.

Soon, people were reaching out to us, instead of the other way around.

The calendar was filling up.

The brand was growing. My passion for the work was clear. And I didn't have to share the success or the control with any larger company. Missing out on Malaysia was a blessing in disguise, as I got to completely shape the direction of my mission and take the reins on the impact I wanted to have.

(Does this mean I can claim the president of Malaysia as an Undercover Angel?)

A core tenet of TILL360 is this simple truth: I fight for kids. Intensely. It's not just a brand identity or a slogan on our T-shirts. I mean it!

I want it—my trait of fighting for kids—to come out in *everything* I do, and as I've alluded to several times, it's a huge part of the success that I have seen over the last twenty years.

However, upon reflection, it's the thing that has gotten me into trouble on as many occasions as it has brought me a reward.

I long ago stopped apologizing for this trait (another trait of mine is caring a lot about what others think of me), but I am constantly trying to rein it in so that it serves instead of overwhelms me.

You see, although I've been around this earth for nearly forty-five years, and although you would think I have figured this out by now, trust me (and every youth basketball referee in the state of Minnesota), I have a *long* way to go.

Just ask my kids.

Defensive Dad to the Rescue

In a recent round of middle-school basketball try-outs, my son got cut from the team. Not just from the A team, or the B team, or even the C team. He was, among a handful of other hoopster hopefuls, one of the kids who got cut altogether.

Look, I know what you're thinking. But I promise—I'm not one of *those* parents. I don't bring a clipboard and coach from the sidelines. I'm capable of recognizing my kid's strengths and potential areas of growth. I can (usually) remember that I'm watching an extracurricular that builds character, not the NBA finals.

However . . . Finn is a pretty good player! We *all* thought he was a lock. And worst of all, he was crushed.

I'm not harboring any ambitions of my kid getting a full-ride scholarship or a Nike shoe deal. I know that his placement on a middle-school squad won't impact any long-term career prospects.

But I hate seeing my kid disappointed. I hate watching

him get ostracized from a group of great friends that he's been balling with for years.

Under the guise of seeking feedback so that my son could keep improving his game, I asked the evaluators what their rationale was.

(I know, I know.)

The feedback was short and completely unsatisfying to me. One of the main critiques was that my son had "weak defensive communication."

What?

He's ten!

As far as I'm concerned, the only on-court communication you need at that age is "I'm open!" and "Good game."

Instantly, I felt the parts of me that are competitive flaring up. Middle school Joe, who thought himself a basketball pro and would have been devastated to be cut from the team, was screaming, "Put me in, coach!"

My fingers flew across the keyboard as I typed my response. They wanted defensive communication? I'd show them defensive communication.

After I finished my mega-angry magnum opus, I decided to have my wife look it over. I was hoping she'd perhaps add a few commas, perhaps change my email signature to "best," instead of "kick rocks."

Instead, she said:

"You can't send this."

One of the best parts of marriage (besides having someone to proofread your emails) is that you have double the skill sets from which to draw. While my "I Fight for Kids" spirit was steering the car, Jess's foresight and thoughtfulness was able to pump the brakes.

"This isn't going to change his placement on the team, it's only going to further burn the bridge. You're still going to see these people, even if it's not on the basketball court."

I thought about it. She was right, of course. On

basketball game days, these guys were known as "Coach." On every other day, though, they were people who lived in our community—one was the dad of one of my kid's best friends! I would sit near them in the bleachers for baseball and inevitably run into them at the grocery store.

On my own, I would have concluded that middle school basketball was the perfect place for my competitive and protective instincts to shine.

As it turned out, I was the one who needed to be benched.

Care More vs. Care Less

I know I've just shared a bunch of memories of where my intensity has hurt me, but there are plenty of stories I could share where it's helped me.

As you may have gathered from the above story, I intensely love my kids. What I've learned is that when I can channel that intensity into the right places, it allows me to have a much stronger impact.

Recently I had a conversation with my teenage

daughter, Sophia, as we were walking our dog through the woods. She was sharing a typical feeling that all of us have had throughout our high-school years. There are kids in her class that were, in subtle and not-so-subtle ways, giving her a hard time.

"I'm just trying to be myself, but I get dirty looks from people who just don't like me."

"What don't they like?"

"I don't know! I'm not being mean to kids. I don't make fun of kids. I'm honestly just trying to be myself!"

In total dad mode, I wanted to rage right alongside Sophia. I wanted to tell her to just ignore those kids, that they're just jealous, that she shouldn't care what they think.

And I believe all of that! Sophia is bright, funny, and quirky, and there isn't a single thing that I would change about her.

At the same time, though, I could tap into the feelings

of high school Joe and know how useless all of that advice was.

I hated hearing it from my parents and other adults when I was a kid. It seemed impossible to do, and it felt like too simplistic of a response. Telling anyone to simply "not care" what other people think runs contrary to a human condition that none of us can really avoid.

It's like telling a kid not to scratch a mosquito bite that itches *so bad*. Or telling a little leaguer to just "shake it off" when they strike out with the bases loaded and the game on the line.

We all care what other people think of us. We have a deep-rooted need, as humans, to be part of a pack. Psychologists even theorize that the reason we care about what others think comes from survival instincts.

The inner caveman in all of us knows that if we aren't part of the group, we might not make it. We won't have a spot at the fire. The foot-powered Flintstones car will leave without us!

But I didn't even need to go as far back as the Stone Ages to empathize with Sophia. I could think about middle school Joe, who was insecure about his weight. I could think of high school Joe, who stopped being able to play sports and stopped seeing where he fit in.

I could even think about the Joe I try to forget about—the one who often stood by silently while kids were teased just like Sophia . . . or those moments when I even did the teasing myself.

Suddenly, these moments of insecurity and shame that I tried to suppress and leave behind had a purpose again. Back in those days, I would've hoped that my lowest moments had nothing to do with my legacy.

Now, I was able to tap into those moments to better serve Sophia—one of my favorite jobs of all.

"I hate that classmates are trying to make you feel that way," I told her. "I remember exactly what that feeling is like, and honestly, it's something I still struggle with."

Sometimes knowing that you're heard and understood

is enough. But the protective dad (okay, and the motivational speaker) in me took it one step further.

"I'm not going to tell you not to care. We all care! But I am going to tell you that we need to care less about what certain people think of us, and care more about what other people think."

Sometimes it's easier to start a new, positive habit instead of stopping an old one. We can't order ourselves to stop caring, but we can make sure that we're placing weight on and spending time with positive feelings, as well.

Just as we can draw on positive and negative traits, we can choose how much we tap into positive and negative opinions. You may not be able to block out the bad ones, but you can decide which ones you use to define yourself.

Like, if a random stranger on the street doesn't like how I dress, or walk, or talk . . . that might bother me for a moment.

(Especially because me being aware that the random stranger doesn't like me would mean that they, I don't know, yelled at me as I walked by? Held up a sign? Which honestly just sounds a little embarrassing.)

If, on the other hand, my wife were to tell me that I was acting completely out of line, I'm more likely to take her thoughts into consideration.

And unlike the aforementioned street heckler who hates my fashion taste, the example with my wife is a *little* less hypothetical.

Love You!

Taking stock of your future legacy starts by taking stock of your current and past self.

What are your superpowers? How have they served you? What lives on the other side? How has that hurt you?

The knowledge about yourself that you will gain is worth the time you'll spend thinking through this.

And if you don't know the answer to those questions, I suggest doing one of three things.

1. Tap back into that childlike wonder and awe, and

remind yourself of the things that you used to wear like a badge of honor.

2.   Notice where this superpower has led you astray.

3.   Care less about what random "others" think, and care more about what the people who love you the most think of you.

Finally, look in the mirror. Flash that power pose. And take stock of the amazing, incredible, superpower-filled human that's looking back at you.

That amazing human is filled with…

so much good
so much potential
so much positive energy

that NEEDS to be shared with our world.

But ALL of this impact in the future starts by taking stock of everything you are now!

Friends, when we can see the good, we start believing in that good. And when we believe in that good, we cultivate the confidence that is needed for us to share that good.

Caveman Wisdoms: Legacy Edition
Take Stock

Many times after a speaking engagement, I receive messages from students. Although they vary in nature, there are common themes that are generally repeated.

One of those themes centers around happiness. Or rather, the lack thereof.

If you read the first book, *Just Look Up*, you might remember a story with the confident-on-the-outside/insecure-on-the-inside middle-school girl named Allie.

Though Allie tried to convey her toughness, it was pretty clear that on the inside, there was a little girl who had been stuffed down years ago.

At some point *all* of us stuff that voice down. And I get it. We're busy. We don't have the same time that we once did to make shapes out of clouds, or jump into random puddles, or do any number of things our younger selves did.

In my experience, the happiest people in the world are the ones that spend a copious amount of time doing the things they love the most. It seems like our happiness and spending quality time on what we value are strongly interconnected.

Here's a quick activity that will shine a light in this area for you!

It's called "I Stand for This," and here's how it works (visit **www.JustLookBackBook.com** for PDFs that you can use!):

- **Step 1:** Find a list of around one hundred values (type "list of values" into Google).

- **Step 2:** Of the one hundred or so words, pick twelve that resonate the most with you. These are words you would want someone to say about you if they were to describe you to someone else.

- **Step 3:** Now that you have twelve, you need to be more discerning. Get the list down to your top six.

- **Step 4:** You're probably gonna hate me for this, but now, get it down to your top three.

- **Step 5:** Once you have your top three, write them

down. Post them in plain sight, where you will regularly see them.

Putting these words in a spot where you can see them daily ensures that your brain/heart/soul will be reminded of their importance.

Every time you make a choice that's aligned with one of these three values, you get one step closer to happiness.

Want to take this a step further? Let's look at how to make this a habit with a simple trick you can do every day.

Start every morning with five pennies in your right pocket. Each time you make a choice aligned with one of your personal top-three values, move a penny to your left pocket.

It's a tiny but tangible reminder to help you build choice after choice that's in sync with who you want to be, and what you want to be remembered for.

Post-Logue

Some books have references or glossaries or even recipes at the back. But if we opened with a pre-epilogue, you know we had to "end" with a post-logue.

I put "end" in quotes, of course, because this is really just the beginning.

More of a prologue, if you will.

Finishing the book gave you all the tools, but the question is . . . what are you going to do now?

Actually . . . maybe a recipe *would* help with this.

Think of these five keys as the base ingredients for your favorite cookie recipe.

We're all leaving this book with the flour, sugar, butter, vanilla, and eggs!

What you do now is decide exactly what kind of cookie you're making.

Maybe your cookie has peanut butter—an "Undercover Angel" ingredient if I've ever heard one.

Maybe you'll embrace your inner "maker" and be generous with the chocolate chips. Or maybe you'll be a "faker" and add raisins.

(You've already read the whole book, so I'm not afraid of ostracizing the raisin lovers.)

The point is—you have the ingredients! Your oven mitts are on! The oven's already preheating, so you better get going.

Maybe I'm just hungry, or *maybe this is your moment*.

The way you use each of these principles, think about your journey, and chart your legacy will look different than my method. It'll look different from your neighbor's or your coworker's or your classmate's or your dog's.

The people around you can be used as inspiration and allies and community. But you should never compare one legacy to another. The most exciting part of a legacy is that it's your way of making a difference!

You can't have "difference" by copying your neighbor.

I recently had a conversation with my father-in-law that really stuck with me. He's one of the most diligent, hardworking people I know, working long hours doing manual labor. Basically, for years he's helped to dig the holes that electrical poles go in.

The only reason you drive past those poles without fear of them tipping over onto your car is that they're *deep*.

It's hard, admirable, and honest work. But recently, he said something that shocked me.

"Joe, I think what you're doing is really cool."

Okay, this isn't the part that shocked me—he's a really nice guy! But then he said . . .

"Sometimes I wish that I could've done a job like

yours. It's crazy thinking about how you get to do something that impacts so many people."

I couldn't believe it.

"Without electricity, there's no lights! There's no microphone. There's no impacting anyone," I told him. "The work you're doing makes *my* work possible!"

Too often, we view our legacies in isolation. But legacy isn't just about what you're doing or what you did. It's about what you made possible. It's about who you brought with you.

And *that's* going to look different for everyone—thank goodness.

Leaders, Take the Wheel

I wish I could say that this book is the definitive guide that will help you navigate any problem and create the perfect legacy.

Unfortunately, reading my book isn't enough to ensure that.

You'll also have to follow me on Instagram, @JoeBeckman.

(Kidding, kidding.)

While I'm extremely hopeful that this book will be a useful companion as you continue building your legacy, it can't do all the work for you.

The good news? You're already building your legacy! You're building it every day.

The bad news? They're not all going to be good days.

When you start feeling like you're going off-course, however, the key is to remember that you're still in control.

It's never too late to switch directions. It's never too early to reread this book and get some encouragement!

You're not in this alone, but you are in the driver's seat.

Perhaps this calls for one last story . . . and one last shout out to my old friend Clint.

When I was fifteen, I wanted to do everything my older siblings did.

That was mistake number one—we've already gone over not comparing yourself to others.

When you're a teenager, however, you'll do whatever you can to be cool and fit in. On one particular day, my parents had left me home alone with my siblings. They were, of course, busy doing Older Sibling Things (which can never, ever include the youngest sibling by definition), and I decided I wanted to have a friend over.

I didn't have my driver's license yet, but I had started driver's ed. I figured that I would *turn* sixteen in the time it took to convince my brother to pick up Clint, so I hatched a plan.

Me: Let me take your car.

Matt: Absolutely not.

Me: I'll be so quick!

Matt:

Me: It'll be good practice!

Matt:

Me: If you don't let me, you'll have to pick up Clint!

Matt: Okay, fine.

Score!

The drive to Clint's house went fine. The trouble started when he got in the car . . . and suggested that we pick up some girls from Edina, a fancy suburb about fifteen minutes from ours. It was our ultimate opportunity to impress. What other fifteen-year-olds could pick you up in their car?

The girls hopped in the car, and then the party really started.

But so did the rain.

We were driving aimlessly, listening to music and pretending we weren't completely out of place in this fancy town. With each lap, the streets became more slick and my windshield wipers worked harder.

Eventually, we pulled up to a red light . . . and the car continued right through it. I may have been new to driving, but I *knew* I was hitting the brake. The wet roads just didn't care.

We skidded through the stop and I panicked, knowing I was breaking the rules. Without missing a beat, I threw the car into reverse.

Right toward the bright lights of a cop car.

The car fell silent. We turned the music off.

"I'm so dead," I whispered.

The cop approached the window. His face quickly showed his suspicion as he peered in at four terrified fifteen-year-olds.

"How old are you, son?" he asked.

This was an easy question! I knew the right answer!
"Sixteen."

He gave me a grim smile. "And can I see your license?"

"Um . . . I left it at home."

He arched an eyebrow at me. "I'm going to need you to step out of the vehicle and come with me to my car."

A million questions raced through my mind on the slow walk to his car.

Am I going to jail?
Would going to jail be worth it if it means that mom and dad can't ground me?
Do girls really like bad boys?
And then . . .

Are all my relatives who say I look just like my brother right?

Suddenly, I had a plan.

Now . . . I'm not going to say that I lied about my

identity to a cop, who suddenly believed I was seventeen-year-old Matt Beckman and deserved to be let off with a warning.

And I'm not going to say that sometimes, in pursuit of our legacy, we take unconventional routes . . . including those that skirt around the law.

There's something here, though! My teenage law-breaking was a part of my legacy—it serves as useful analogies for helping others!

(Or at least that's what I tell myself.)

Sometimes our journeys don't go exactly how we planned them.

Sometimes we want to slam on the brakes and throw things into reverse.

But no matter how stuck you feel, or how much you think you've messed something up, it's never too late to rechart your legacy, reclaim your life, and become someone new.

Fifteen-year-old Joe took that literally. But we can all do that in little ways!

By shedding the things—physical and emotional—that don't serve us any longer, and adjusting to the time of life in which we are currently, we Seize the Season.

By looking down less and looking up more, we will notice where our kindness and compassion can lead us to be someone's Undercover Angel.

By tackling the times in our lives where it feels like we have nothing to do with enthusiasm instead of dread, we Embrace Boredom.

By thinking consciously of how we want to be remembered and what we want our legacy to be, we Meet Our (Inner Difference) Maker.

And by loving the parts of ourselves that have gotten us this far, and avoiding the opinions that don't matter, we Take Stock.

And if you ever feel downtrodden,
or forget how far you've already come,

or are considering driving in reverse without a license but you don't know whether or not a cop is behind you,

Just
Look
Back.

Till360

Inspiring Educators • Supporting Leaders
Engaging Families • Fighting For Kids

All schools want to create a positive, equitable, high-quality instruction and collaborative environments for students, staff, and families. But many schools cannot meet those needs because they don't have the necessary support systems.

Our TILL360 team collaborates with and works alongside district leadership and school sites to develop the internal capacity to integrate specific processes, procedures, and practices that support social, emotional, and behavioral growth.

Through an MTSS Framework, Till360 helps school communities build a welcoming and supportive environment where students and adults create meaningful human connections (for their hearts) so learning can actually happen (in their brains).

We get to work first by listening to understand YOUR

goals, YOUR initiatives, and YOUR pain points (every district is unique!), and the result is a personalized school plan with a scope and sequence that will be sustainable after we're gone.

"TILL360's dynamic speakers are masters at sharing authentic and powerful stories. EVERY person in our audience (young and old) was able to understand they are not alone on their journey, and the single best way to move forward is with each other."

—Lori Zimmerman, Director of Professional Learning with the Minnesota Association of School Administrators

If you're a . . .

- School leader looking to improve the culture in your building

- Conference organizer looking for an award-winning keynote for your next event

- School district looking for long-term help around larger systems and practices

 Send a message to
Info@TILL360.com!

About the Author

Human. Connection. Matters.

As co-founder of TILL360, Joe Beckman's mission has been to **RECLAIM HUMAN CONNECTION** in educational communities throughout the world.

Over the last twenty years, Joe has shared his infectious energy, humor, and passion in over 2,000 schools, and has positively impacted over 1 million people through . . .

- live speaking events

- powerful videos

- and through his best-selling book, *Just Look Up: Five Life-Saving Phrases Every ~~Kid~~ Human Needs to Hear*

Joe resides in Minneapolis, Minnesota, with his four children and exceptionally beautiful, patient, strong, and kind-hearted wife, Jess.

Book Joe to Speak!

Over the last nineteen years, Joe Beckman has spoken in educational settings all over the world with one simple mission: to reclaim human connection.

If you're looking for a . . .

- Conference keynote

- Professional development training

- Student session

- Parent or community event

Visit Joe's website at www.TILL360.com

"Bottom line . . . if you're looking for a speaker to engage, motivate, and genuinely connect with your crowd, Joe's your guy. This is the highest recommendation I can give."

—Jennifer Tiller, Chief Academic Officer, EducationPlus

"Joe's great in front of kids, and he's even better in front of educators. Every time I go to his presentations I leave inspired."

—**Hal Urban, Author, Life's Greatest Lessons**